ALPINE PASSES OF SWITZERLAND
Journey to Modernity

In *Wilhelm Tell*, his verse drama dated 1804,
Friedrich Schiller extolled the impressive beauty
of the Gotthard Pass:

Ascending still you gain the Gotthard's heights,
On which the everlasting lakes repose,
That from the streams of heaven itself are fed,
There to the German soil you bid farewell,
And thence, with rapid course, another stream,
Leads you to Italy, your promised land.

Translation T. Martin, 2001

ALPINE PASSES OF SWITZERLAND
Journey to Modernity

Carène Foundation

Contributors Anton Affentranger
Daniel Lätsch
Doris Leuthard
Frédéric Möri
Richard de Tscharner

Scheidegger & Spiess

CONTENTS

Preface   7
Doris Leuthard

A History of the Alpine Passes   9
Frédéric Möri

The Pass as a Source of Spirituality   51
Frédéric Möri

Photofolio I   85
Richard de Tscharner

Alpine Passes and Their Strategic Importance in the Past and Present   159
Daniel Lätsch

A Vision and Project of the Century   173
Anton Affentranger

Photofolio II   183
Richard de Tscharner

Afterword   209
Richard de Tscharner

Photo Captions   217

Historical Maps   229

Contributors   249

Carène Foundation   253
Guy Vermeil

Acknowledgements   257
Richard de Tscharner

L'aurore à la Furka – Furka Pass (Uri)

FOREWORD

Doris Leuthard, Swiss Federal Councillor (2006–2018)

These beautiful artistic photographs of Swiss Alpine passes and the rare narratives accompanying them invite us to contemplate the role of the passes in the momentous and often poignant changes that have shaped our country over the ages and to our day.

Since time immemorial, the passes have served as connecting points between regions, people and cultures. Constantly exposed to harsh weather conditions and coping with climate change as best possible, the passes retain their unifying role and our fascination. Though they have been conquered and made accessible by man, Nature's greatness, to which we remain beholden, commands our humble reverence.

In recent decades, energy-producing sources such as reservoirs, wind turbines, pumped-storage plants and solar installations have been constructed on or around many Alpine passes in Switzerland. It is our responsibility to strike the right balance between the advantages of generating more energy and the importance of preserving the natural landscape, while remaining ever mindful of respecting the environment when it comes to human intervention. There remains potential for new installations, which would indeed be welcome where the energy is as locally produced and renewable as possible. Nevertheless, rationale in their favour must be considered with care and weighed seriously against their limitations.

For a long time, the Alpine passes served as commercial trade routes. This role has evolved with the increase in mobility, technical progress and the opening of the Alps to new modes of transport. The numerous tunnels that have been built reduce distances, save time, make routes safer and allow travel all year round. With tourist travel and accident rates rising in the summer months, it is reassuring to have the option of alternative routes, both open pass roads and tunnel connections.

Freight and passenger traffic have increased to such a degree in recent decades that they could not have been managed without tunnel connections. When it comes to mobility, our country has always given due consideration to the natural environment. Not only have we built the world's longest rail tunnel, but with the "Alpine Initiative" adopted by the Swiss people in a referendum, seeking to protect the Alpine regions from the negative effects of transit traffic, we have also played a pioneering role in shifting heavy transalpine traffic from road to rail. Debate about protecting the Alps has raised awareness among the Swiss population while politically ensuring, overall, the promotion of less polluting lorries, the greater use of rail transport and a sophisticated transportation redundancy system between road and rail – with hubs as far away as northern Italy. This transfer policy can be described as unique on the European scale, having a significant effect on the entire transport strategy and protection of the Alpine region. European transport corridors are increasingly oriented towards reasonable coexistence of road and rail options as well as the protection of the Alpine region.

The opening ceremony of the Gotthard Base Tunnel on 1 June 2016 was a great success. The presence of German chancellor Angela Merkel, French president François Hollande, Italian prime minister Matteo Renzi and many more dignitaries testified to the European significance of our undertaking. In the run-up to the event, I invited not only the transport ministers from the Rotterdam-Genoa EU corridor but also representatives of transport companies such as the German Deutsche Bahn (DB), the Swiss national railway (SBB/CFF/FFS), the Italian national railway (FS), the French national railway (SNCF), and the Port of Rotterdam, among others. Bringing together all the parties concerned was vital. The best infrastructure is meaningless if it is not used to move as much freight as possible, in coordinated fashion and in concertation regarding maintenance work, the reporting of any incidents and so on. Cooperation, exchange of information and the application of common standards are essential to a successful transport policy.

Our passes remain crossroads, meeting points and strategic locations. They now primarily serve regional, slow and redirected traffic, and leisure activities. For many cyclists, reaching the top of a pass is the goal of summer tours. Families plan their road trips through passes and are delighted to be able to stop at a mountain restaurant or spend the night in a hospice. Alpine farmers sell their cheese, flowers and other products to travellers. Let's make sure we take good care of our marvellous Alpine expanse and ensure a modern transport policy.

A HISTORY OF THE ALPINE PASSES

Frédéric Möri

The morning of the seventh day

The Alps emerged on the final morning of the world. The awesome alternation of jagged peaks, valleys and Alpine passes emanate from the last orogenic process that began more than 66 million years ago and is still ongoing. They form part of an array of alpine topographic reliefs extending from Morocco to China via the Balkans and the Carpathian, Taurus and Himalaya mountains. This range results from the thrust of the Arabian Peninsula, Africa and the Indian sub-continent toward Eurasia.

Various links in this long mountain range are occasionally subject to earthquakes, each such occurrence reminding us that the Earth is forever evolving in a timeframe not of our making. Even more impressive, up to their very peaks our Alps reveal traces of the prehistoric Tethys Ocean, which covered what is today known as Europe over 250 million years ago. To anyone able to discern the clues observable in fossils and salt deposits, today's peaks, vertiginous slopes and rock formations signal that this was once an immense oceanic expanse populated by antediluvian creatures.

The Alps present a paradoxical landscape: mountains symbolize the epitome of stability, yet the seemingly stationary Alps – stationary only to our eye – in fact show the constant movement of the Earth's crust. While appearing now to already belong to the heavens to which they majestically rise, to the initiated eye the Alps overtly expose the utter recesses of the Earth: the various geological strati beneath us – predominantly verdant on the Swiss plateau – are fully exposed, somewhat like an inverted abyss. Their distribution is the work of the massive and ongoing labours of the Earth: from a mass of granite that reaches from the Lötschberg to the Gotthard, the Alpine arc spreads out in a myriad of shades of sandstone and limestone, bordered on the north and south by a fringe of sedimentary formations set apart from the Alpine range as the result of erosion. Each displays unique hues of grey, white, ochre, green, and more. In terms of the Earth's timeframe, however, the striking diversity represents a mere flash instant in an otherwise continuous evolution.

The climate, too, has evolved continuously, presenting significant variations even within the relatively short time of Man's presence on Earth: between 7400 and 4900 BC, the snowline was 300 metres higher than it is today. The successive periods of hot and cold weather conditions continuing through to our own time have been largely determining factors in the development of human societies. The warmer periods enabled colonization of the highest mountain pastures and the mobility of goods and people via Alpine passes at high altitudes. They mark the heights of cultural, economic and political development, in particular Rome and the Roman Empire, the first Renaissance lasting from the eleventh to the thirteenth century, the Industrial Revolution and the rise of liberalism after 1860. In contrast, human development stalled during the colder episodes as evidenced by the fall of the Roman Empire, the invasion of the Barbarians and feudalism (fifth to tenth centuries), the political upheaval and decline in the fourteenth century, and so on.

Ephemeral places

The Alpine passes bear the vivid markings of this ever-evolving human presence. Recent studies reveal that around 4000 BC, hunters, merchants and shepherds regularly crossed the Lötschberg Pass linking Valais with the Bernese Oberland – a pass not used in colder times. Rome annexed the Great St Bernard Pass during a favourable warmer period, and built a road and a sanctuary on that high ground. Yet it was in the midst of the Little Ice Age that the Bishop of Turin decided to build a refuge (or hospice) there, which proved indispensable to enabling passage all year round. For centuries, the Theodul Pass, at 3,200 metres, became a significant and regular point of crossing between the Val d'Aosta and Valais, as evidenced by the many period coins that have surfaced after thaws. In another instance, warming temperatures recently exhumed the body of a Swiss mercenary who died of frostbite while attempting to navigate this same pass around the year 1600. No one would have attempted such an ambitious undertaking at the start of the next century and ultimately, irretrievably covered by ice, the pass was lost to posterity.

Invitation: dare to venture

Alpine passes grace the greater part of Swiss territory: 2,187 passes have been named and of these 120 are today serviced roads. Half are in the Alpine cantons of Grisons and Valais where the highest of the passes, the Silbersattel, is located at 4,519 metres. The large number of passes in the country suggests that, contrary to presenting a barrier, the area of what is today Switzerland is first and foremost a point of passage, unlike the Pyrenees or the Himalayas.

In his encyclopedia, Berliner Johann Georg Krünitz (1728–1796) defines a mountain pass (from the German word *Pass*) as both "a narrow and difficult passage, notably from one country to another", and "an invitation to continue one's journey freely". In other words, the invitation is to forge on, regardless of the obvious challenges to passage. Men and animals alike have taken up that daunting challenge. No other mountain range of such considerable expanse and importance is as well suited to the circulation of life. The paradox concisely expressed in the German definition rather accurately describes what Switzerland would indeed become.

Arrival of settlers

Seasonal encampments in caves in Simmenthal, Valais and Eastern Switzerland dating from the Middle Paleolithic period (50,000 BC) mark the oldest signs of Man's presence in Alpine heights. The oldest traces of sedentary settlements in the valleys date from the Mesolithic period or Middle Stone Age, around 8000 BC. Relics of a hunters' encampment from around that period were discovered on the Italian flank of Splügen Pass, above 2,000 metres. The progressive integration of the Alps into the great European bartering network began then, as evidenced by objects discovered from both northern Italy and the Celtic regions to the south and east of the Alps. Such traffic was, however, limited.

Strategic locations

The Alpine passes indeed remained hostile environments difficult to navigate until the beginning of the Christian era. According to the Roman historian Strabo, the route leading to the Great St Bernard Pass was at the mercy of the Salassi, a violent tribe of looters who ransomed travellers, most often as they neared the summit. To make matters worse, the passage itself was "gruelling and narrow", prohibiting transport of any goods. There are indications that most of the major Alpine passes were controlled by extortionist "tribes", but the routes were more or less well maintained by local villagers who venerated their tutelary deities on high, at the summits. This was the case at the Great St Bernard Pass, where a temple was dedicated to the Celtic god Penn.

Axis of the Empire

The Roman era presented a turning point. Alpine passes had long been a danger to Rome, which ultimately fortified all access points to them. Though merchants were able to pass unhindered, the territory of Valais was closed to the Romans from the Great St Bernard Pass to the Furka Pass. This obstruction to their political expansion posed a real threat to the Romans. Gallic tribes descended on northern Italy from the Alps around 400 BC and a mere ten years later, from these provinces in northern Italy, they struck and ransacked Rome. Legend also has it that it was from the Great St Bernard Pass – one of the larger passes – that Hannibal's troops descended in 218 BC during the Second Punic War, although in fact it was more likely from the Little St Bernard Pass. The threat had shaken the mighty Roman Empire to the core. Crossing the Alps, Hannibal suffered the loss of a good number of his men as well as the elephants accompanying them. But his passage stunned the powerless Romans who appeared petrified before a leader capable of such an inconceivable act. They suffered defeat after defeat before finally succeeding in overcoming the onslaught *in extremis*. Later accounts by Greek historian Polybius and Roman chronicler Livy confirm the highly perilous nature of the crossing. The absence of practicable routes, the hostility of the tribes controlling the passes, problems with water and food provision, the harsh climate and the phenomenally steep grade of the slopes proved prohibitive for large, heavily burdened groups. A century and a half later, in 57 BC, Caesar himself failed in his attempt to secure the route and was forced to abandon the pass to the Salassi before proceeding to conquer the Gauls.

It was only in the first century of our era that this major pass was finally conquered, controlled and shaped by the Romans in keeping with the state they intended to build. Emperor Augustus brought the Salassi to their knees and ordered the building of the town and fortress of Augusta Pretoria (Aosta) to guard access to routes to the south. A stone-inlaid road 3,70 metres wide, in some places chiselled into the rock itself, defiantly crossed over the heights, making it possible for heavily laden mules to carry wares along the route relatively safely. Emperor Claudius had the entire circuit paved in the year 47, rendering it more roadworthy and enabling passage once the snow had melted. Holes in the rock near some summits suggest that Roman engineers had provided planks to facilitate the passage of beasts of burden and perhaps even carts on terrain that was otherwise unstable in poor weather conditions.

Though covered by additions dating from the Middle Ages, the ancient route is still visible today on both flanks. Finally, a sanctuary and shelter at the summit offered resting places for weary souls and bodies. In the same year, Claudius's romanization of Octodurus (Martigny) fully secured the route and sealed Roman establishment in the valley. Penn was replaced at the summit by Jupiter, the tutelary deity of Roman power and thereafter over the Alps.

The Roman presence now extended over more than 70 km between Aosta and Martigny – a considerable distance for that time. Until then there had not been any comparable investment in a mountain pass, nor would there be for years to come. In this same first century of our time, Roman emperors had made the Julier, San Bernardino and Septimer Passes operable, effectively integrating them into the vast network of Roman roads. To the north, they provided direct access to Limes Germanicus, the Empire's fortified boundary, which had to be constantly defended against Germanic tribes. Routes in the Grisons area were used more frequently by mercenaries than merchants. Today it is virtually impossible to find any trace of Roman presence on those routes, unlike the Great St Bernard Pass, which was infinitely better equipped, connecting as it did the new conquests of Gaul and Britannia with Roman Italy, and further, via the Peninsula's ports, with Egypt, Greece and Asia. The pass is situated at the very heart of the diagonal that connected the confines of the Roman Empire with its core. For the first time ever, an Alpine pass located in today's Switzerland played a crucial role of major strategic consequence for the entire continent. Other major Alpine passes would subsequently follow suit in this strategic respect, and so to this day. This brought upheaval. A transit industry developed, bringing financial gain for the population, once it had been integrated into the Empire. The locals reorganized their means of livelihood, becoming muleteers, guides or purveyors of food and wine, yet all the while preserving their local specificities. The Valais region is a case in point: though the Romans made peace with the descendants of the "semi-Germanic" tribes mentioned in the Livy chronicles, they never completely assimilated them. Nonetheless, romanization of the Great St Bernard Pass deeply impacted "Helvetia", as what later became Switzerland was then called. Romanization is, indeed, one of the major pillars of contemporary Swiss identity.

Dark ages and renaissance

The second pillar of Swiss identity derives from the successive migrations of Germanic populations that put an end to the Roman Empire. Crossing the Alpine passes repeatedly, they pillaged Rome and settled permanently in a good portion of what constitutes Switzerland today. Roman infrastructure collapsed with the Empire: little was left of their roads, merely sparse sections poorly or barely maintained. Security and the volume of traffic declined substantially. This phase of insecurity and precariousness coincided with a general cooling of the climate, mentioned earlier, leaving the Alpine passes far less practicable for some time to come, and hindering economic development in the region's valleys.

A new political order gradually developed with the spread of Christianity in the Western world, Christianity being the third pillar of Swiss identity. The Church of Rome succeeded the Roman Empire by introducing a dense network of bishoprics throughout Europe, reminiscent of the tightly controlled administrative order of Roman times. The City of St Peter again became a prime destination for pilgrimages and a new bastion of universal power. At the same time, the prince-inheritors of Germanic potentates wielded increasing civil power, and slowly mobility resumed locally and regionally. From the ninth century on, circulation grew significantly at the Gemmi, Furka, Lötschen, Grimsel and Oberalp Passes. Each of these marked a border between potentates, by now firmly established and determined to increase their wealth through commerce and trade.

To endorse the legitimacy of his new empire, Charlemagne crossed the Great St Bernard Pass after his coronation in Rome by Pope Leo III at Christmas in the year 800. He made Rhaetia an independent county directly subject to his administration. The territory of what is today modern Switzerland regained its strategic importance, and this time in two ways: the Alpine passes ensured control over passage between the Germanic and Frankish territories, heartland of the restored Empire, and also between the spiritual and political centres of the Church. The Church, however, having developed since the fourth century and grown considerably wealthier in manpower and financial means, was intent on controlling these roads and proceeded to create an increasingly dense network of abbeys, hospices and resting posts. To a significant degree, the Church was master of the passages until the Renaissance. Disentis Abbey, founded circa 750 at the entrance to the Grisons region, was placed under the authority of both the Emperor and the Pope – which was highly symbolic in and of itself – but it was in fact run by the ecclesiastics. Saint Maurice Abbey, Switzerland's oldest abbey, controlled exclusively by the Church, commanded the strategic Great St Bernard crossing and the transversal link between Rhaetia and Geneva. As such and through to today, the network of hospices and abbeys in Switzerland represents this third pillar of Swiss identity: the Christian influence.

The Saracens

The flourishing Carolingian empire and the infrastructure renewal it provided did not last. Charlemagne's continental edifice disintegrated, initially dividing into three distinct kingdoms as of 843 (Treaty of Verdun), each of which was then divided into more or less autonomous entities before further splitting into duchies, counties, baronies and so on. By the turn of the tenth century, all centralized governance had disappeared, and in some instances, there was no rule at all beyond town boundaries and the castle towers of local overlords. Roadways were neglected and insecurity grew, dramatically at times, prompting travel in groups – and even that was not always enough to ensure safe and sound arrival. The Saracens, distant descendants of the Salassi, arrived in Valais in 920. They controlled the Great St Bernard Pass and destroyed the Hospice at Bourg-St-Pierre, the only hospitable rest stop for travellers at the time. They robbed and ransomed travellers of all stations in total impunity, randomly plaguing most of the Alpine passes in Valais for more than half a century. They did the same below, pillaging the Saint Maurice and Disentis Abbeys in 940, known to be depositories for the riches transiting via the Alpine passes, a portion of which was converted into valuable objects kept in the abbey sacristies or "treasures".

Cluny Abbot Majolus was sequestered near Orsière (Valais) in 972 and freed only on payment of a ransom of 1,000 silver coins, a phenomenal sum for the time. Chronicles hold that the Saracens treated "him and his Bible" with utmost respect. Still, all of Christendom was taken aback by his imprisonment, for it blatantly signalled the severe degree to which circulation in the Alps had become dangerous, while at the same time reaffirming its utterly crucial role, even at its worst moments. At the time, the Cluny abbots were considered even more powerful than the Popes in Rome. They ruled over a flourishing spiritual and financial empire. Their expeditions into Roman territory, in person, were vital to the well-being and development of ecclesiastical power, the sole transnational entity at the time, and as such, the embodiment of economic, cultural, intellectual and spiritual unity and stability on a continent in the throes of total disintegration. The sequestration of Majolus and his release by ransom were undoubtedly instrumental in bringing about conscious awareness of this in the courts of Europe.

A man of God and world order

It was in this context that Saint Bernard of Mont-Joux (circa 1020–1081) entered the scene. Pitying the pilgrims and travellers, or so the story goes, this son of high-ranking nobles from Aosta is considered to have rid the western Alpine passes of the last remaining Saracen gangs. He restored the infrastructure at the Little and Great St Bernard Passes, building hospices there around the year 1045. He brought live-in clerics there to serve as guides, monks, hosts and roadmen. Perched at the highest point of the great pass – at an altitude of 2,743 metres, at the foot of Mont-Joux – the Great St Bernard Hospice, many times rebuilt, still stands today, overlooking the Combe des Morts. In the bleak and rocky landscape, it conjures the image of a lighthouse exposed to the most extreme weather conditions.

Without questioning Bernard's sainthood in any way, his achievements nevertheless also served political and economic ends. In keeping with the custom of his time for the younger sons of high-ranking nobility, he became a monk and distinguished himself as such with the support of a strong network of family alliances and feudal ties. He was related to Ermengarde, the last queen of Burgundy, who had received Bourg-Saint-Pierre in dower. Bernard decided to double the facilities by adding a hospice at the summit. Donations flowed in from the bishops of Aosta and Sion, and probably also from prominent families in these valleys and even beyond. With this endowment he restored the two major roads in the western Alps on which the prosperity of the northern part of the Italian peninsula partially depended – the future Grand Duchy of the West (Burgundy), the Holy Roman Empire and the Kingdom of the Franks. Situated as they were at the very interspace between the realms of the great powers of the time, the two Alpine passes that would later bear Saint Bernard's name were duty bound to remain open and never to become completely dependent on any one side. After Bernard's death, the Great St Bernard Hospice would expand its influence over great distance throughout Europe, from

The Great St Bernard Hospice and the Mont Vélan

Clearing of the Great St Bernard Pass road by the Hospice canons

England to Sicily, in the form of a network of hospices, hostels, priories and churches, totalling eighty-six in the year 1286.

Once the Great St Bernard Pass had become sufficiently secure, it was no accident that Bernard served as a mediator between the Pope and the Emperor during a famous meeting in Pavia in 1081. Symbolically, Switzerland's policy of proposing its good offices dates to this occasion, implemented by those who kept the Alpine passes open regardless of the sometimes blood-letting rivalries that alternately opposed emperors, the kings of France and England, and the dukes of Savoy for supremacy over the Alpine roadways. Donations from all poured in generously to ensure the upkeep of this dense network of facilities which the Church alone could supervise from its lofty position above and beyond the uncertainties inherent in international politics. From the eleventh century on, what would ultimately become Switzerland was profiling as a place of passage whose reason for embracing neutrality would gradually become clear to all.

Expansion

Bernard and his successors achieved their triumphs in a context of wide-ranging global expansion, in all dimensions. From the eleventh and notably twelfth centuries, a period of global warming facilitated agricultural development in all of Europe along with the significant population growth, the development of towns, and growing prosperity for monasteries, princes, merchants and, to a greater or lesser degree, peasant farmers.

New economic clusters emerged and developed around trading centres. In northwest France, bustling trade fairs in the province of Champagne attracted all of merchant Europe to a vast emporium where the rarest and most sought-after goods were openly traded all year long: oriental spices and silks, fabrics and household linens from Flanders and England, manufactured products from Spain and amber from the confines of the Holy Empire. The attractive meeting and innovation opportunities the fairs offered drew all who mattered in the world of trade – to chart commercial strategies, make connections needed to ensure provision of supplies, and seal alliances and partnerships.

The East held an instrumental role in the medieval economy, particularly for access to coveted Chinese silks and Indian and East African spices bought at high price by Arab merchants. The three republics in northern Italy – Pisa, Genoa and Venice – ensured the supply of these precious goods for all of Europe before Venice ultimately won the exclusive prerogative for this. The shortest route from Alexandria to Troyes in Champagne led through the Great St Bernard Pass, via Genoa and Venice.

Large-scale transalpine traffic resumed in the twelfth century, calling for improved infrastructure of the Little and Great St Bernard Passes to enable the transit of goods from Alexandria and Malacca. Merchants also soon took to reopening the old mule trails and Alpine passes in Central Switzerland and Grisons. The trade fairs in Champagne dominated affairs until the end of the thirteenth century, before giving way to exponential economic development in northern Europe, from Flanders to the Baltic Sea, fuelling pressing demands for quicker routes to Germanic locations from northern Italy. During this period the Septimer, Julier, Majola, Splügen, Lukmanier and Furka Passes were re-equipped and frequented, in some cases, nearly year-round.

More than ever, the Alpine passes represented high stakes. The roads to access them were hotly disputed by the Ottonian emperors, the Hohenstaufen, the Dukes of Savoy, the bishops of Sion and Chur, while the Dukes of Zähringen and local high nobility with them established Alpine seigniories. Throughout all this time, Alpine passage was safeguarded by the clerics, ever mindful never to take sides. The Knights Hospitallers of St John of Jerusalem (a Catholic military order) built a hospice at the summit of the Simplon to crown the importance of the passage they had secured for the first time. The monks continued to build houses and priories along the road to the Great St Bernard Pass while the great St Maurice and Disentis Abbeys in effect annexed the Alpine regions to the major political and economic European networks. Control of the land in the valleys leading to the passes, or even of the Alpine passes themselves, alternated between warring factions and for varying lengths of time. But it was always the men of God who safeguarded the Alpine crossings and for this reason these were never at risk. However complex the array of tightly knitted alliances and feudal suzerainties playing out at the time – and the complexity remains baffling to this day – the race for power over the passages indicates that the Alpine environment was largely and sustainably revitalized by the time of the flourishing renaissance in the twelfth and thirteenth centuries.

Empire of Alpine passes: Berchtold V of Zähringen

Berchtold V, Duke of Zähringen (1160–1218), established his economic powerhouse in the Pre-Alps. Having developed the cheese-making industry in the Bernese Oberland and beyond, he aimed to become master of the commercially promising routes to Italy on one side of the Alps and to the Germanic, Burgundian and French domains on the other. Transporting goods was costly, and harshly taxed by all the local overlords on whose territory the roads passed. The Alps had cut him off from Italy, curbing his expansionist intentions. In 1211, he marched an army over the Grimsel Pass in an attempt to conquer Valais for a foothold there to secure passage to the south. He had mastered passage of the Gotthard, but the Reuss valley was too difficult to manoeuvre, prompting his risky campaign in Valais for direct access to the Great St Bernard and Simplon Passes. As recorded, he was defeated by staunch Valais peasants in the battle of Ulrichen in the Goms valley (Vallée de Conches); his disbanded troops backtracked over the Grimsel Pass to return to Bern or Fribourg. His first strategy amiss, Berchtold then set his sights on the Gotthard; he took charge of the shores of Lake Lucerne (Vierwaldstättersee) and control of major routes, and attempted to make passage over the Schöllenen Gorge practicable, but the steep terrain and the Reuss river's turbulence made this extremely challenging. His incursion into Valais probably gave the duke occasion to meet the local population, the Walser, and to admire their building skills and techniques. These highland peasants, as inherently insular as can possibly be on account of the staggering terrain of their surroundings, excelled in the construction of Alpine infrastructure, challenging as that was in their environment: they specialized in building bridges, roads tacked onto steep mountain flanks, irrigation ducts (*bisses*) in improbable places – no challenge seemed too great for them. Berchtold employed them and commissioned works that no one before them would have dared even imagine. The House of Zähringen died out in 1218 for lack of an heir. But had it not, the rulers of Bern, Fribourg and Central Switzerland might have mastered a large portion of the road linking Bern with Italian-speaking Ticino, and so-called "primitive" or Inner Switzerland could have been founded under a reigning family. Like the Savoy, it would probably have been entangled in transalpine conflicts. The extinction of the Zähringen line had perhaps significantly influenced the nature and destiny of this state-in-the-making. This point has not been given its full due.

Opening of the Gotthard, Act I: the Walser feat

The Walser were mountain peasants originating from Upper Valais (*Haut-Valais*). From the end of the twelfth century, they emigrated in small groups and colonized lands that had devolved to the state by escheat in a radius of some 300 kilometres, from the Chablais to the Kleinwalsertal regions in the northeastern part of Grisons. Their migration within the Alpine arc testifies to the mobility of populations at the time and, more broadly, to the socio-economic upheaval that characterized the medieval renaissance. Their role in the development of the Gotthard area is well known. The access point in the north is the daunting Schöllenen Gorge, bypassed by means of muleteer paths scaling the Bäzberg or Riental. The steep ascent severely restricted carriage of any load and lengthened the distance to Andermatt considerably. For this reason, international traffic transited essentially via the Alpine passes in Grisons or Valais. Of the Walser undertakings, posterity has notably retained construction of the *pont écumant*, renamed the Devil's Bridge (*Teufelsbrücke*) as of the sixteenth century. It was an unbelievably daring achievement, perched above an abyss of torrential waters, defying a hellish landscape of rock and foam. They also built a long path affixed to the rocky slope, held in place by a support system the shape and structure of which resembled the irrigation ducts for which the Walser were known. These took much longer and were technically infinitely more challenging to build than the Devil's Bridge. The path wound alongside the rocky wall of Kilchberg through to Andermatt valley.

Shortly after these Walser accomplishments, in 1230 the Bishop of Milan built a hospice at the Gotthard Pass and renovated the sanctuary. As such, a combination of spiritual and road facilities marked the opening of the way. In those times, when the majority of people had faith, no one would have dared venture into such hostile terrain without the benefit of saintly protection. Gotthard of Hildesheim (960–1038), a Cluny monk and exceptional preacher, had been a prestigious figure. With his relics enshrined in the hospice chapel, serene passage was guaranteed to the men of the time.

For a long time, the cliff bordering the eastern shore of Lake Uri prevented travellers from taking the most direct route from Schwyz to Göschenen. This perhaps explains why the Gotthard remained a pass of secondary importance until relatively recent times. It is known, for example, that at the turn of the sixteenth century an average of only 170 tons of goods were transported annually by this route compared to 4,500 tons transiting via the Brenner Pass. Initially, the Gotthard's significance was regional: it had made possible the development of Central Switzerland and that of Basel and the Milan region. At the turn of the fourteenth century, some twenty commercial firms in Lucerne were working regularly with partners in Milan and Como. Central Switzerland owes its rapid growth at the time to the Gotthard, which culminated in the constitution of the first of the Swiss Leagues united by "oath" at the end of the thirteenth century. The pass gradually grew in importance, as the fourteenth-century conflict for its control between the Swiss Leagues and the Bishop of Milan testifies.

**Birth of a Confederation:
Switzerland by the people, and by passage**

The first alliances were formed on the north flank of the Gotthard, eventually leading to the first "Confederacy", established in 1351, assembling the cantons of Uri, Schwyz, Unterwalden, Lucerne and Zurich. Its core unit was the initial league that had united the cantons overseeing the Gotthard: Uri and Schwyz, allied to Nidwalden as of 1291. They sealed their independence by defeating the Habsburgs at Morgarten in 1315.

Such alliances were not uncommon between Alpine territories, which swore each other mutual assistance while retaining their independence in matters of internal politics. There were other such alliances in the same period in the Dauphiné region and in Grisons. By extending to the Plateau through alliance with Zurich, and shortly thereafter with Zug and Bern, as of 1351 the new "Confederacy" included both a passage through the Alps and extensive pre-alpine territory, the combination of which gave it singular political and economic strength. The confederated cantons had in fact made the Duke of Zähringen's dream come true.

The political history of Switzerland could therefore be said to have originated around the Gotthard, in symbolic terms at least. A pluralist state, its essence has always been to act as a buffer while maintaining its independence *vis-à-vis* the great political and economic powers that its vocation has been to bring together. From this posture, which essentially originates in the function of the Alpine passes, Switzerland derives its prosperity and legitimacy. As guarantor of free passage to neighbouring powers, from which it benefits,

Switzerland must remain neutral per se. The neutrality will seem all the more authentic where it is not subject to the authority of a duke or prince, boisterous types more often than not, and rarely content with the limitations of their domains; their mission is indeed to expand them. On the contrary, the state is governed by a sovereignty that is shared between the urban bourgeoisie and the "peoples" of the valleys and plains all regrouped around communication links, independent and proud of their distinctive identities. It is in their interest to maintain an equilibrium between them and to flourish and grow wealthier by maintaining and operating the commercial arteries. It would be their ruin to attempt to enlarge their realm by engaging in any transalpine confrontation. Once the Austrian threat had been eliminated, this particular posture constituted a key factor of the Confederates' success, as it had from the very outset.

Another key to their success lies in the geography. Within the Gotthard range, a longitudinal crossroads links Grisons and Valais via the Furka and Oberalp Passes and a transversal axis directly links the Rhine Valley and the Po Valley via the Schöllenen Gorge and the Gotthard Pass itself. In the Andermatt valley, the route linking the Habsburg lands with those of the Great Duchy of the West and France crosses another route linking the Germanic Holy Roman Empire with the merchant Republics of Italy and the Papal states. Moreover, the Gotthard is located at the crossroads of the four linguistic regions of what would later become Switzerland and the principal rivers that have their source there. For a long while, the Gotthard was considered the highest range in Europe. These symbolic facts came into full measure only in the nineteenth century and particularly in the twentieth, when the Gotthard came into its own as the distinctly crucial feature in the identity of a considerably larger country. The opening up to international traffic created economic conditions for the emergence of a singular state, corresponding to what is today Central Switzerland.

King of Simplon

The Renaissance, the Italian Wars and the expansion of the Habsburg empire in the sixteenth century placed the Alpine passes more than ever at the crux of the political chessboard on which the great powers played. During the Thirty Years' War the passes retained their function as vital places of passage for the Imperial powers, facilitating troop mobility from one front to another.

After the Walser, another famous clan played a leading role in the design of Alpine passes from the end of the Middle Ages to the classical period. The Stockalpers originated with the Olteri family in Milan. They settled and acquired land around the Simplon thanks to the good graces of the Duke of Savoy. In the fourteenth century, they secured their permanent establishment in the Alps by adopting the name of a locality on the road to the pass – Stockalp. Over the centuries, their political influence and prosperity grew to the extent that they became one of the most prominent families in Valais. In the seventeenth century, in the midst of the Thirty Years' War, a certain Kaspar Stockalper (1609–1691) obtained from the Duke of Milan the privilege of transporting goods on the Simplon road and later, a monopoly on the commercial trade of salt and other valuables such as resin and larch polyphora, used in pharmacology. He also exploited mines and founded transport companies that operated along the major routes in the area – hence also on the Alpine passes. To improve connections and accelerate delivery of supplies to the Milan area, he began to renovate the Simplon Pass. These were colossal works in their time: the full distance of the packhorse path was virtually rebuilt and in places even redesigned, and it was reinforced with engineering structures and dotted with inns. Though still not a carriage road, it nonetheless afforded the best possible craftsmanship and conditions of its time. The overall result brought the Simplon route up to par in quality with the Great St Bernard and the Gotthard, thus tripling the international transit opportunities on the territory of what is Switzerland today. Stockalper razed the old Hospice of the Knights Hospitaller, also known as the Order of Knights of the Hospital of Saint John of Jerusalem, and in its place built a more imposing structure which to this day dominates the small plain over the road on the south side of the pass. Sign of the times: the Church ceded its predominant role at the pass as private entrepreneurship gained ground. It was said that when Stockalper travelled, he would reserve the upper floor of the hospice for himself, returning to his family roots in Alpine simplicity and the rugged rocky landscape at the grandest of Alpine passes.

Stockalper was no ordinary man. He exemplified an early and well-documented incarnation of an exceptional nature that is rather particular to Switzerland: the innovative entrepreneur heading an enormous fortune, town councillor and political figure, benefactor and builder, he had "connections" to the great courts of Europe whose interests he managed to serve without betraying anyone. He was probably one of the very few men of his time to be designated Knight of the Golden Spur (Papal states), Knight of the Order of St Michael (France) and Knight of the (Germanic) Empire at the end of the Thirty Years' War, which had opposed those three powers in one of the most terrible wars that Europe had ever known. His work on the Simplon Pass made him a precursor of the man who would later build a tunnel through the Gotthard, Zurich's Alfred Escher, but he surpassed Escher in international stature and perhaps also in terms of the renown that he contributed to winning for Switzerland in particularly trying times. Stockalper was dubbed the "King of Simplon". Overlooking the town of Brig, his power base, the size of the palace he built there mirrored the extent of his power. Three monumental towers topped with gilded onion domes crown the main buildings of colossal proportions, as though to signal that coherence and integrity are rewarded with affluence.

Viable roadways and modern Switzerland

A revolution occurred in the next century when the Canton of Bern launched a vast programme of viable carriageway construction (1742). Conducted on a grand scale throughout the entire country, the construction of these facilities in essence marked the first transport revolution, before that of the railways. These works demonstrated unprecedented state (cantonal) engagement. The system of mandatory public service that had prevailed until that time obliged local inhabitants to contribute to road maintenance, albeit not always with satisfactory results. This was replaced by salaried work and the introduction of public management of construction and maintenance services that renewed and modernized all the major thoroughfares in the country; these were opened to private entrepreneurship shortly thereafter. Once regular water drainage had been secured, the roadways could be used all year long, day and night, reducing travel time by a factor of two or even three, and encouraging the introduction of efficient postal services and the development of transport companies. These achievements, which lasted nearly a century, allowed Switzerland to enter the age of modernity.

Battle for the Gotthard

Understandably, roadway development at the great Alpine passes took a longer time than down in the valleys or on the Plateau. Revolutionary wars underscored their need, however. Engaged in a conflict against the

The Old Hospice and the Barral House at Simplon Pass

Simplon Hospice and Monte Leone, 3,565 m.

Second Coalition, France clashed with the Russians and the Austrians on Helvetic territory. Following terrible confrontations near Airolo and on the Tremola slopes, a fierce battle opposed a French division and an army of Russo-Austrian troops commanded by Russian General Suvorov on 24 September 1799, at the most vulnerable point of passage known as the Devil's Bridge. The Russians dominated in the frontal clash that took place at the bridge deck. To this day they celebrate this victory in uniform and with fanfare before a monument they erected at a bend in the former road. They were nonetheless ultimately defeated on the Plateau and chased out of Switzerland by the French, who remained masters of the passes until the end of the Empire (1815). This battle demonstrated to all and sundry the strategic importance of passes, as though it still needed to be shown, but it also illustrated the degree to which the access roads were still problematic.

To commemorate this short-lived victory the Tsar commissioned a painting by Alexandre von Kotzebue, *Suvorov's Troops Crossing the St Gotthard Pass in 1799*. It depicted the inadequate and precarious transport infrastructure. Haggard, weary troops are shown filing along a shabby path that can barely be made out, preparing to cross the torrential river on a surprisingly narrow bridge. In the forefront, mules carrying cannons and chests of munitions also prepare to cross. There is no carriage in sight to relieve either men or animals of their burden, nor is there any sign of carriage-mounted artillery. This looked more like an expedition in the demi-wilds of North America, as portrayed by Chateaubriand in the same period. On the left, a group of soldiers departs from the narrow path to climb up the mountain: the old road is not up to carrying the weight of a modern army. Though the artist clearly exaggerated his strokes to emphasize the courage of the men and the adversity of the elements in their ordeal, the pass as depicted harks back to another age, hostile and hardly practicable. This was also precisely how Chateaubriand and William Turner depicted it, crossing there a few years later before the pass was transformed into a carriage-worthy road.

Simplon, the first strategic European pass

Development of the first carriage-worthy road began the following year, in 1800. It was initiated by Napoleon Bonaparte, victorious in Switzerland following a previous victory in Italy. Victorious on both sides of the Alps, he ordered the construction of a wide road for vehicles at the Simplon, designed for bi-directional passage of cannons and heavy military vehicles. This first modern transalpine road was decidedly military by design, guarded by an army stationed at the pass and reserved essentially for its exclusive use. Studded with engineering works and later with a hospice of unusual proportions, large enough to accommodate entire military companies, the new roadway proved that it was possible to make an Alpine pass viable within a limited time span. Of course, it became an outpost of primary importance in the emperor's strategy, enabling the opening of the shortest and fastest itinerary between Paris and Milan. From this outpost, France's *Grande Armée* could attack the Habsburgs from the rear at any time and descend on the Austrian plains in record time.

The Devil's Bridge (Teufelsbrücke) and the Schöllenen

Schöllenen Gorge

The Emperor and the Great St Bernard Pass: pious images

This was the second time that Napoleon conquered the Alps. The first, due to courage and tenacity, was won when he led his army across the Great St Bernard Pass in winter conditions, in May 1800. The second was won at Simplon, where technical and engineering prowess allowed for decisive progress to be made in the design and construction of transport infrastructure fitted to the demands of the time. A regular stagecoach service was inaugurated in 1805. In winter, passage was guaranteed by means of sleigh-drawn vehicles until 1954, when systematic snow removal was introduced. Simplon was the first and only Alpine pass to be equipped with infrastructure designed to enable passage at all times, in all conditions. It was the ultimate strategic pass if ever there was one.

In the same period, in 1806, the emperor launched somewhat more modest though nonetheless substantial roadworks at the Great St Bernard Pass. The pretext for this was his wish to erect a monument in the hospice church in tribute to General Louis Charles Antoine Desaix (1768–1800) where his remains were buried to commemorate his victory in the Battle of Marengo during the Italian campaigns. This required building a navigable road so that the lavish monument could be transported. Its placement at the summit of the pass was a strong political statement, confirming France's control of the historic pass in symbolic terms. And in practical terms, too – by doubling traditional access from the west, the new road to the pass added to the symbolic significance.

Still in this period (1805), the emperor commissioned the famous painting, by Jacques-Louis David, of himself on a horse, exhorting his troops as they crossed the Great St Bernard Pass in 1800. The rather unusual composition of the scene veers from the right to the left, to which Napoleon forcefully gestures with his finger. The pass to be conquered is on the left. This inverted orientation to the left, generally considered to be ominous in Western culture, invites interpretation as victory over adversity, as the successful reversal of the course of things by the will of one man alone. In the scene as set, the Alpine pass represents the impossible feat to be overcome. There are no fewer than five original versions of the painting, all by David himself. Engravings were reproduced and widely circulated throughout the newly established Empire. This first official image of imperial propaganda exalted the heroic virtues of the freshly crowned general for his crossing of the Alps and likened him to Hannibal, victorious over the elements and set to repel the enemies of France nestled in the Po Valley. This was thus a double victory. His strong hold over the Alps symbolized the universal power that nothing could resist. The image was propaganda at its finest, because in fact Napoleon's army behaved crudely, requisitioning, stealing and damaging property, and never compensating anyone despite General Bonaparte's promises. This was labelled "the spoils of war". Still, the painting largely contributed to imprinting the legendary stature of the Great St Bernard Pass in the collective conscience. Alas, neither these images nor the new road to the Simplon Pass were to benefit the emperor: the last army ordered to march across the Simplon Pass consisted of 80,000 Russian soldiers who invaded France in 1815, attacking the French from behind and precipitating Napoleon's downfall, after his previous defeat at Waterloo.

Paved roadways

Between 1805 and 1840 the roads leading to the major Alpine passes were made accessible to vehicles. The San Bernardino, Splügen, Gotthard and Julier Passes were equipped to allow passage of stagecoaches and transport wagons without damage. This was revolutionary and caused the most remarkable mutations prior to those to come later with the automobile. The McAdam paving technique, named after the Scottish engineer who designed it, was the predominant paving method until the 1950s. Efficient and regular maintenance of the roads significantly increased traffic.

The most emblematic of the developments during this period took place at the Gotthard, yet again. Beginning as early as 1707, engineer Pietro Morettini blasted the first tunnel through the Alpine rock at the Reuss Gorge. This feat, using explosives and aided by local inhabitants in the Urseren valley, marked the first shift in the balance of power between man and the pass, even though it cost the lives of two workmen. For the first time ever, man had acquired the power to overcome the might of the mountain at its very core and impose his will. The famous "Uri Hole", 64 metres long, two metres wide and 2.5 metres high, resulted in the abandonment of the Twärren Bridge, which was too narrow and too difficult to maintain. This was a considerable breakthrough, but the mule road remained obsolete on both sides. Consequently, between 1827 and 1830, engineer Francesco Meschini designed plans for a modern route over the

Simplon Pass road through the Gorge at Gondo

Simplon road, Kaltwasser Gallery

Schöllenen Gorge, below the Uri Hole, building a new, wider and higher Devil's Bridge, as well as a paved road chiselled into the mountainside the full distance linking the bridge to Göschenen. He also equipped the Hospental road, which edges its way between the masses of rock up to the top of the pass, and the Tremola road on the southern slope. The Tremola road is famous in its own right, for good reason: even today the serpentine climbs 300 metres in altitude around twenty-four hairpin turns – each of which has its own name – bordered by retaining ramps up to 8 metres high. Monumental structures support the vertical foundation of the road, measuring up to 7 metres in width at the widest turns, providing relative security for the coaches. The granite paving, which has lasted to this day, guarantees the road's stability and durability.

Thanks to this novel infrastructure, a daily stagecoach service was initiated and, with sleigh-drawn postal services, could function regularly, even in winter. Boring of the Axenstrasse roadway fully opened up the Gotthard on the north in 1865: this monumental effort enabled the road to Basel to wind along the rocky slopes overlooking Lake Lucerne. In the same decade, the routes to the Furka and Oberalp Passes were also modernized, eventually making the Gotthard the ultimate crossroads of Switzerland, and of Europe. From 1870 and until the inauguration of the Gotthard railway tunnel (1882), some 70,000 travellers and 20,000 tons of goods per year transited through the pass. During this short period the passes were at the peak of their glory before the dawn of the modern era, considering the numbers of passage and the nature of the transit so essential to both national and international traffic.

In the years from 1860 to 1880, Alpine passes continued to play the role they had always played, though on an unprecedented scale during this time, shaping as it did a veritable reverence of the passes in the Swiss collective consciousness. As often occurs, however, peak was soon followed by decline.

Conquering the pass:
Alfred Escher's contribution

The 1850s were a turning point in European history. Following the "People's Spring" (1848), economic liberalism gradually gained ground and the Industrial Revolution was in full thrust. It was somewhat hampered by slow railway development, then only in its embryonic stages, but that development quickly became a priority throughout Europe, if only to deliver the coal and steel needed in the large industrial centres that were taking shape.

The need for a transalpine railway connection was obvious from the start of the decade. An initial project through the Gotthard was launched in 1851. To the most lucid observers, despite the modernization efforts under way the roads to the passes were outdated because they could only be navigated by horse-drawn carriages. Among them, Alfred Escher (1819–1882) seems to have understood this better than anyone since he gradually but unwaveringly set up a "system" that would enable the establishment of a transalpine link via the first railway tunnel under the Gotthard Pass.

Born into the upper bourgeoisie in Zurich, Escher was first and foremost a leading politician at both cantonal and federal levels. His project seemed to aspire beyond merely introducing a new railway line. His aim was to ensure that these colossal construction works became the vectors of Swiss economic and technical development. Switzerland was lagging considerably at the time. Escher founded Credit Suisse, the first share-held investment bank, and the first insurance company of national significance, the future Swiss Life. He personally assumed the presidency and supervision of both institutions. In 1857, France started work on the Mont-Cenis tunnel. Taking this into account, Escher figured that the Swiss tunnel should pass by the east, connecting Germany with Italy. Escher presided over the founding of the Federal Institute of Technology in Zurich. Ultimately, he founded the Gotthard Railway Union, aiming to coordinate efforts at the federal level. Fifteen cantons participated in this endeavour. After heated debate, he succeeded in having the final itinerary pass through Zurich. He founded and presided over the Swiss Railway Union and, personally leading the negotiations, obtained endorsement of the rail itinerary by Italy and the German Empire as well as their financial contribution to the project in 1871. It was a promising time: newly created on the ruins of the French Empire, the German Empire had a financial fortune comprised of war indemnities at its disposal. A speculative bubble was created, and Europe started booming.

Well aware as he was that any construction delays and cost escalation would mean the project's economic failure, Escher entrusted its implementation to Geneva engineer Louis Favre. Favre committed to completing the work within eight years and to paying a late fee of 5,000 francs per day thereafter, doubling that amount in a second year of delay. He sought out the labour and material resources that had recently been used in the boring of the Frejus tunnel in France. Escher was at the height of his glory when the drills first resounded in Göschenen.

The undertaking proved to be unbelievably complex. Building a transalpine rail line at that location involved perforating three spiral tunnels on the north ramp, around the village of Wassen. In all, the project comprised fifty-six tunnels and ninety-five bridges. Moreover, no preliminary geological studies were then available to help measure the difficulties that the workers would encounter at the core of the mountain in building the 15-kilometre main tunnel, the longest in the world at the time.

These challenges took on alarming proportions. Delays accumulated on account of the nature of the rock at the site of the main tunnel but also, as could be expected, on account of the quantity and type of engineering works set to feature on the north side. Working conditions were horrific: a total of 177 workers, mostly Italian, lost their lives working on the facing of the main tunnel alone. The workers went on strike in 1875; this movement ended in bloodshed. The massive use of dynamite didn't improve working conditions to any degree; in fact they became worse, causing an epidemic of silicosis among the workers. Construction costs for the main tunnel exceeded initial estimates as early as 1876. The speculative bubble had burst, and Europe was in crisis. Supplies for the site were difficult to come by and subsidies became inevitable. It was in this context that the people of Zurich refused their "prophet" Escher extension of credit. He was forced to resign from the presidency of the Gotthard Railway Company in 1878. The following year, Louis Favre, whose health had been declining rapidly, died while on a visit to the Göschenen construction site. The railway tunnel was finally opened on 28 February 1880, less than eight years in the making. The tunnel was delivered on schedule, but Favre was dead, and Escher was not invited to the tunnel opening event, nor did he attend the inauguration of operations in 1882, the year of his death.

A king deposed

Alfred Escher was indeed the architect of the Gotthard line and as such, one of the founding fathers of modern Switzerland. His accomplishments amount to a colossal feat. In essence, he enabled Switzerland to continue to pursue the role that it had always made its own: to be the mainspring of European interconnectivity and exchange. By virtue of what this vocation implied for the time, his achievements profoundly transformed the country and raised Switzerland to the stature of a modern state in terms of economic and infrastructure development. The technological prowess so dearly acquired during construction of the rail line would allow Switzerland to continue its modernization by building other transalpine tunnel passages – Simplon opened in 1906 – and also dams.

Escher brings to mind Kaspar Stockalper, the "King of Simplon", who had succeeded in making that Alpine pass a major thoroughfare for transalpine traffic in the seventeenth century, contributing to the economic development of that part of the country. But the "Tsar of Zurich" or "King Alfred I", as he was derided, was never crowned "King of the Gotthard". The year after his death, his friends had a monument erected in his honour at their own expense, and the city of Zurich, which owed him its leading position in the Swiss economy, just barely consented to financing upkeep of the monument.

This disavowal is partially due to the difficulties that arose during construction. It is primarily due to the strong opposition by a part of the political class in the 1850s. Unlike Stockalper in the seventeenth century – to whom the cumulative effect of wielding both political and economic power was attributed in his time – Escher was not credited with the same in his. The Industrial Revolution was in full motion by then, and political liberalism and economic liberalism were advancing at the same time. On a more profound if less conscious level, by forcefully birthing modernity in Switzerland, Escher put an abrupt end to an era that the Swiss would soon come to idealize – the Switzerland of Alpine passes.

Flüela Hospice, 2,388 m., and the Schwarzhorn, 3,150 m.

At Furka Pass, postcoach and the Hotel Furka

Rhône Glacier, general view of the Grimsel and Furka roads

Death of the passes and the "vicissitudes of a nation's soul"

In his captivating book, *La poste du Gothard ou les états d'âme d'une nation* (2015), author Peter von Matt points to the timely concurrence of the Gotthard tunnel opening and the notoriety of a painting celebrating the famous St Gotthard postal coach that had been crossing the pass daily since 1830.

The painting by Rudolf Koller was commissioned by the Swiss Northeast Railway Company (*Schweizerische Nordostbahn* or *NOB*) and presented as a gift to Alfred Escher in 1873, the year in which railway tunnelling was at its most intense. To date the painting remains one of the most vivid representations of Swiss art, not so much for its purely aesthetic qualities as for the poignant message it would seem to convey.

The circumstances depicted leave little doubt as to the intended interpretation, at first glance at least: the stagecoach is hurtling down the ramps of the old Tremola road, startling a herd of cows and nearly crushing a calf in passing. The contrast between the motions of the coach and the horses, "frozen" as the coach manoeuvres a sharp turn, and the confounded gaze of the onlooking cows, produces a dramatic effect. The artist had immortalized on canvas the features of a world that the new tunnel had condemned. The painting could be considered as an ode to "progress" – and to its most representative paragon, the pioneering Alfred Escher – by enterprising men conscious of the far-reaching implications of Escher's work from its start. And so be it if that world was meant to disappear, for that road and mode of transport presented dangers and problems highlighted in the painting at a time when Europe was in the throes of the Industrial Revolution and building railway infrastructure on a grand scale.

Like all important works of art, however, Koller's painting invites several interpretations. Already in 1873, the postal coach symbolized the emotional attachment of the Swiss to the most famous of their Alpine passes. And Koller's portrayal emphasized a stark reality: the coach and speed are seemingly out of place in the bucolic setting, compromising its peaceful composure. The artist's last-minute addition of the calf accentuates the violent aspect of the scene, adding symbolic resonance: innocence and purity, values the Alpine setting embodies, are brusquely threatened by the breakneck speed of the vehicle. And the symbol is reversed: the double-barrelled message might also illustrate – who knows – progress-in-the-making, destroying in its wake the ancestral traditions dearly cherished in the heart of Helvetic identity as captured in this idealistic depiction of the most emblematic Alpine pass of all. Interestingly, reproductions of the painting widely circulated after the opening of the Gotthard railway tunnel in 1882, which also marked the end of the postal service via the pass. The painting became a well-known marker in popular Swiss imagery celebrating times of yore. The success of this "icon of the good old days" is paradoxical in that it tolls the bell of the very era that it celebrates, while announcing a new dawn.

Peter von Matt points out that the painting echoes the reflections of Basel historian Jacob Burckhardt (1818–1897). He developed the concept of "historical crises", which holds that "an economic crisis tends to coincide with an unprecedented acceleration of speed in history and civilization". In this context, the acceleration was spurred by the French defeat in 1871 and the subsequent financial bubble, which burst in 1873. That resulted, within just a few years, in a surge of globalized trade and the abandonment of the realms of art and reflection in favour of business ventures. The arts and intellectual activity in general became "merely a branch of commercial activity". Local traditions declined from then on and "a serious regression of national custom was observed in intellectual output".

Koller's painting illustrated the tense dynamics that had developed at the core of Swiss identity from the 1870s onward as the result of the sweeping changes in the world that had begun in the 1850s. In their wake, the Gotthard had become an integral feature of Swiss cultural history and occupied the crucial place that it would retain until the mid-twentieth century as the symbol of an evolving nation whose identity was to be situated somewhere between an archaic past and a modernity into which Escher had brutally precipitated the country by dint of pneumatic drilling.

Transformation of the passes: tourism

The opening of the rail line signalled the end of the Alpine pass as a necessary point of passage and each new tunnel opening hammered home this reality more forcefully. Passage at the Simplon plummeted from 13,258 travellers in 1905 to a mere 845 in 1907. In just two years, the Simplon ceased to be a transit hub and, for growing numbers of people, turned into a destination of choice for leisure activities and exploration.

Beginning in 1850, the British took to the Alps, and to mountain climbing. Their founding of the Alpine Club in 1857, consecrating "alpinism" as a sport, introduced a new perspective on the Alps. Neither scientific nor poetic but sports-oriented, it bespoke a new relationship with the surrounding environment reflecting the scientific fervour that had overtaken the continent.

In a few decades, tourism would become the mainstay of Switzerland's valleys and Alpine passes. The English had come to equate Vacation = Switzerland = the Alps. The interconnectivity of the various railway networks operating on the continent in the 1860s and 1870s greatly facilitated tourist travel. A new type of edifice emerged in Europe – the hotel, typically situated at the foot of Alpine passes when not at their summit. In 1857, Alexander Seiler bought the Gletsch Inn at the road-crossing between the Furka and Grimsel Passes and proceeded to turn it into the Grand Hotel Glacier du Rhône, one of the most famous and appreciated hotel complexes in Switzerland. Slightly higher, the Belvedere Hotel opened in 1882 on the Furka Pass, allowing well-to-do tourists to admire, from their hotel rooms, the glacier sprawling beneath them. At an altitude above 2,200 metres at the summit, the Furkablick Hotel welcomed tourists as of 1893. The nature and function of the old mountain inns were transformed. From the authentic refuge they had provided for centuries as shelter for wayfarers obliged to stop for rest, they became holiday destinations in celebration of the Alps, transformed per se from frightening heights into fascinating sites.

The veer toward tourism was given a further push from the beginning of the twentieth century with the upgrading of mountain roads to meet the needs of automobile use and the introduction of electricity in visitor facilities. Some establishments transposed the architectural volumes and luxurious lifestyle of the great capital cities to the mountains – the former Grimsel Hostel was centrally heated as of 1932.

The development of tourism, typified by the construction of high-altitude hotels, brought a radical upset for Alpine passes in terms of their shape and function. Most no longer served as critical passages from one accessible Alpine road to another, but instead as access points to Alpine leisure and discovery. Places previously feared became increasingly accessible and familiar, as well as symbols of a bygone past. As most passes were fitted for light vehicle traffic, it became possible to explore higher altitudes at lower cost, sometimes taking only an hour or two. The development of national road infrastructure and the technological advancement of motor vehicles reduced travel times; it had become possible to climb up to and over a pass, descend on the other side and return home to the Plateau in time for bed. For motorcyclists, motorists, cyclists and hikers, short exploratory excursions were within reach. Switzerland continued to honour its role as the crossroads of Europe more than ever, though from that point on transit traffic was moved to its basement, in the form of 280 road and railway tunnels.

Simplon, last of the Alpine passes

This major pass in Valais is one of the most important in Switzerland. It has served uninterrupted passage since prehistoric times. Napoleon chose it as a strategic stronghold, as we saw earlier, commissioning the construction of facilities unprecedented for their time, which enabled passage in all seasons. Following the pass's eclipse by the opening of the Gotthard tunnel, and later the Simplon tunnel, like all its major counterparts the Simplon Pass experienced renewed activity with the advent of motor vehicles. But it was the Simplon's integration in the national roadway network in 1960 that most significantly changed its nature as a thoroughfare. Revitalized as a strategic crossing, the only one of its kind in Europe, it was newly designated to be an artery for heavy vehicle passage all year round. This proved to be a useful precaution: following the outbreak of a fire in the Gotthard tunnel in 2001 traffic was rerouted and passage of heavy vehicles over the Simplon Pass doubled. In 2010, 80,000 vehicles crossed the Simplon. The imperatives of year-round availability demanded technical adjustment and colossal construction efforts: a series of monumental bridges (the Ganter bridge towers at 145 metres), covered carriageways and tunnels ensure that traffic remains fluid in all weather conditions. Regular snow removal on the access ramps and on the pass itself are ensured by equipment and know-how that is virtually unique in the world. At the same time, the old Simplon road built by Kaspar Stockalper was rehabilitated, inviting hikers to use the pass in much the same conditions as those who came before them five centuries earlier, with a stop for rest at the hospice built by Napoleon, entrusted by him to the Augustinian order, and still active today. The Simplon thus accrues, in a unique association, the ancestral functions of a pass, facilitating crossing from one slope of the Alps to another, together with its contemporary function as a recreation ground.

T.C.S. excursion by Gletsch, below the Furka Pass, 1913. Cars parked in front of the Hotel Belvédère.

Descending from Furka Pass

Together, the two create a curious chiasmus: the ancestral function, passage or crossing, is fitted with the most modern technical facilities and the contemporary function, leisure, is best enjoyed on foot, along the revived ancestral path. The two ways meet at the summit of the pass, beneath the "Simplon Eagle". This commemorative landmark was erected in 1944 by the 11th Mountain Brigade, using rock mass originally intended to reinforce support of Gondo Fort. It is a reminder of the pass's strategic role during both world wars in the twentieth century. The choice of the eagle as an emblem is rather traditional, but at this particular location, just a stone's throw from the hospice built by Napoleon two centuries earlier, it takes on an ironic, or at least significant twist. Here it marks the explicit appropriation of Alpine passage by the national community, on the very spot where a foreign stronghold had been mightiest and most manifest. In this respect – since the upgrading of facilities initiated there in the 1960s and notwithstanding the reputation of the Gotthard – it could be said that the Simplon Pass is one of the most emblematic representatives of Swiss identity, without any sense of exclusivity intended.

Switzerland, an "island of peace"

The first half of the twentieth century, marked by the First and Second World Wars, is probably one of the most complex and decisive chapters in the history of Switzerland.

The first of these conflicts revealed profound antagonism between the Swiss of Latin and Germanic origins, at times in dramatic terms. These tensions along cultural lines date back to the turn of the century and intensified as of 1909 over the Gotthard Convention. Construction of the tunnel having largely been financed by Germany and Italy, there was a move to buy out the two foreign powers, allied at the time, on the eve of what appeared to be imminent conflict. The convention drafted by Swiss political leaders and economic decision-makers provided advantageous conditions for the two foreign nations. For partisans of national independence, this amounted to a sellout of the Gotthard to Germany and Italy. The Swiss parliament nevertheless ratified the convention in 1913 in spite of opposition to it by a good portion of the population. The incident caused a big stir and, with the war officially declared shortly thereafter, raised consciousness in Switzerland. This resulted in a 1921 hallmark decision – from then on international treaties would be subject to popular referendum. No international treaty would be ratified by the Swiss parliament nor signed by the Federal Council, the Executive branch in Switzerland, without the consent of the governed.

The Gotthard issue prompted the emergence of a movement known as the New Helvetic Society (*la Nouvelle Société Helvétique*), launched even before the start of the conflict. This association of intellectuals and politicians rallied around Gonzague de Reynold, a historian and activist from Fribourg, whose objective was to "strengthen national sentiment" and to "prepare Switzerland for the future". The threat from beyond its borders underscored Switzerland's strategic position. The movement arose in reaction to cultural differences in mentality and to the absence of genuine national unity, as acutely revealed in the matter of Swiss sovereignty over its most strategic Alpine pass. It was at this time that the word *Graben* (rift or ditch) was first used to refer to this internal cultural and linguistic divide in the nation.

The divide became openly apparent during the First World War. Staunchly pro-German, Swiss General Staff officers were counting on victory by the Central Powers and advocated closer ties with the Second Reich. For their part, French-speaking and Italian-speaking Swiss applauded injured French soldiers as trains rolled by from Italy, which had sided with the Allies. The war appeared to be raging in the Swiss conscience, on both sides of the linguistic divide. Germanophile sentiment in military and economic circles in German-speaking Switzerland went as far as collusion in the "Colonels affair" (*Oberstenaffäre*). Two senior officers were accused, justifiably, of communicating Swiss military information to Germany and Austria-Hungary in exchange for sensitive intelligence. Clearly, Swiss military leaders had chosen their camp. But this affair had aroused strong indignation in the army and the French-speaking population. Compounded by the serious social strife sparked by the lack of raw materials on account of the war and the agitation still simmering in the aftermath of the Russian revolution, this cultural divide brought the country to the brink of disaster.

Italy's change of allegiance in 1915 had preserved Switzerland from a likely fatal threat of implosion. Had it remained allied with the Germanic powers, the Gotthard axis would have in effect become the kingpin of the Alliance's military operations, in which case Swiss neutrality would have hardly been tenable and would most certainly have raised severe internal turmoil.

The Alpine passes played virtually no role at all in the Federal Council's defence policy. The only serious concern was over the Plateau, in the north, for fear that German and then French divisions would pass through that area to skirt around adversary positions. This fear was not totally unfounded since the option had in fact been considered by the German military command before finally opting to pass via Belgium. The French had also considered the Swiss option but ultimately, neither command chose to take this route.

Le Largin, located east of the town of Porrentruy in the Canton of Jura, faced the frontline between French and German operations. The famous "kilometre zero" line was drawn there, marking the southernmost point of the war's Western Front that extended up to the North Sea. The Swiss contingent at Le Largin was literally wedged into the no man's land separating the French and German trenches. Not a single shot was fired by Swiss soldiers, but the majority of federal conscripts were stationed there and from that vantage point experienced war firsthand as the belligerent sides engaged mercilessly in that new form of conflict called "attrition warfare".

Its counterpart on the far eastern side of the country in Grisons also left its imprint on the collective consciousness. At the prominent Umbrail Pass, the highest paved Alpine road in Switzerland at an altitude of 2,500 metres, Swiss soldiers monitored the Italo-Austrian border from trenches that were hastily dug when Italy entered the war on 23 May 1915. Here, too, the goal was not to repel an invasion but to prevent any overflow into Switzerland. At this Alpine location, the nature of the mountainous terrain and the belligerents' resources significantly reduced the risk of invasion compared with such risk at the Alsatian border. But the imperatives of neutrality obliged the Swiss army to repel with fire any and all territorial infringement, whatever its source.

There was no shortage of action. Transposed to high altitudes, the war of the trenches was particularly inhuman. At temperatures nearing -30 C degrees in winter, Italian and Austrian conscripts battered each other with explosives and landmines, ran surprise raids wielding knives and generally suicidal attacks led by officers who proved incapable of influencing their respective commands. Some soldiers literally froze to death and combatant troop relief often resembled perilous mountain scrambles.

Here, too, from their own trenches, dug as best they could in the protrusion of the pass, Swiss soldiers remained powerless witnesses of the horrors of modern warfare. They were obliged to fire at Austrian or Italian units that had unwittingly crossed the border, its confines concealed by snow, or who were attempting to flee the furour of combat. In such cases, any territorial infringement could be of a mere dozen or so metres, often to reach a higher, more advantageous firing position. Had Swiss soldiers not fired in such instances the other camp would have considered the border effectively non-existent. This absolute imperative of dissuasive fire, aimed at soldiers who were not an enemy per se, set a challenging moral dilemma before Swiss soldiers. They were also forbidden to assist any wounded between the two enemy lines – again, to avoid risking the accusation of taking sides.

The memorial which, to this day, recalls this improbable episode in Swiss history eloquently conveys the suffering that these men endured. Not only were they powerless observers of the sordid spectacle that was this exceptionally cruel war, but they were also forced to participate in it, as though an enemy of both opposing camps. Neutrality had long been conceived as the backbone of contemporary Swiss identity, but it was forged in those trenches and in the bunkers of Le Largin. Neutrality implies taking an external stance in a given context, all the while being condemned to observe the events and offer refuge to all the belligerent parties equally. This may seem like a convenient position, but it is never easy. On the other side of the no man's land, the men who had fallen spoke the same languages as the Swiss.

It would still be quite some time before this aspect of Swiss identity could be fully defined, but its premise had been made clear. Europe was alarmingly suicidal in 1914, and the position of Switzerland seemed untenable, even unjustifiable to the young men singing songs of future victory in the railway stations of London, Paris, Berlin, Moscow, and later Milan. Four years later, the survivors of the August 1914 offensive attacks no longer considered Switzerland in the same way. Like so many others, the young Ernest Hemingway, who had served as a volunteer on the Isonzo front (Italy) in 1918, experienced the trauma of this first modern war. His romanticized account, *A Farewell to Arms* (1929), offers a singularly poignant analysis of the pointlessness of this new type of conflict, where there is not a chance for manhood or chivalrous spirit. The notions of "glory, honour, courage" are "obscene" to experienced soldiers. To him, the sacrifices on the battlefield "were like the stockyards at Chicago", the only difference being that "the bodies weren't buried".

Frederic Henry, Hemingway's *alter ego* in the novel, finds refuge in neighbouring Switzerland with Catherine Barkley, the nurse who cared for him when he was ill. They lived on the slopes of the Jaman Pass above Montreux, near the Alpine setting of Jean-Jacques Rousseau's *Julie ou la nouvelle Héloïse*. There, Hemingway's characters pull together the life-sustaining threads of their lives, one by one. The setting and the characters on the roads leading up to the pass are not mere decor; they are described in precise detail. And it is no accident that the future laureate of the Nobel Prize for Literature situates his story on a road leading up to an Alpine pass. For members of "the lost generation" Switzerland is no insignificant land populated by men emasculated by peace, cowardly shrinking away from taking an active part in history. It is a haven offering escape from the alienation and the death drive that brought Europe to the brink of the precipice. Though romanticized, the ending of *A Farewell to Arms* attests to reality: some 30,000 wounded from both camps were welcomed and cared for in Switzerland during the First World War.

Mediation and prosperity: "The Spirit of Geneva"

The "island of peace" image became a cliché, literally, for the duration of the war: It was disseminated in postcard format and ultimately made its way to the Ranft chapel in the Canton of Obwalden dedicated to St Niklaus von Flüe (1417–1487), patron saint of Switzerland. The votive fresco in the chapel, painted in 1920 by Robert Durrer, shows an island emerging out of a sea of corpses. Three emperors (the Tsar, the Kaiser and the Austrian Emperor) reign miserably in the sky above, having lost their crowns. Columns of refugees rise out of the pestilential waters to seek refuge on the rock. The island archetype was popular at the time: in his memoirs, Basel psychiatrist Carl-Gustav Jung relates a similar dream he had in 1913. The symbolic image of an island materialized in the shape of the numerous international organizations that have been founded or developed in Switzerland, transforming the country into a kind of sanctuary.

First among these is the International Committee of the Red Cross (ICRC), founded in 1863. The General Postal Union followed in 1874. As of 1878 it became the Universal Postal Union (UPU), where the terms of all postal exchange were established at its headquarters in Bern. These included a provision stipulating that in case of conflict, postal exchange would transit via Switzerland, which thus became a symbolic point of passage, a point of encounter between the most remotely located populations, or those most opposed to each other. These were the first organizations of their kind, allowing collaboration to continue beyond any conditions of conflict. The First World War accelerated the development of such organizations, as it did many other domains. The Swiss Peace Society, the oldest pacifist organization in Europe, was founded in 1917. Considering that Switzerland was spared conflict in the First World War and that it was the seat of international organizations such as the ICRC and UPU, which had played a critical role during the conflict, its founders wanted Switzerland to take a more active role in seeking negotiated resolution of conflicts. Hot in the midst of the "Colonels affair", when the army – and on a broader scale, the population – was grappling with the challenges of neutrality, international circles – not to say "internationalist", for the word can be rather ambiguous – had come to understand that Switzerland had chosen active neutrality as its vocation for the twentieth century. In November 1920, Geneva welcomed the establishment of the headquarters of the League of Nations initiated by Woodrow Wilson. The Treaty of Locarno was signed in 1925 by France, Germany and Belgium to draw the "definitive" borders of peace. Mortified by a war in which there were no outright victors, all of Europe seemed to "embrace the Swiss spirit" in the course of the Roaring Twenties in the sense of adopting a new attitude of collaboration in international relations. "The oldest democracy in the world", as Federal Councillor Giuseppe Motta liked to point out, hosted over eighty non-governmental humanitarian organizations in 1938. Switzerland, more than ever a "special case" (*Sonderfall*), stepped outside the conventional limits of a neutral, or in other words neutralized, state to inspire chancelleries and government offices with what was known as the "Spirit of Geneva" – advocating dialogue, concertation and collaboration – that indeed infused international relations, with the overarching objective being to preserve peace. The ultimate ideal would be to see the world governed like Switzerland.

This political utopia had been heralded by the French pacifist Romain Rolland, which he expressed in now famous words. He found refuge in Geneva in 1914, where he published *Above the Battle* (*Au-dessus de la mêlée*), a peace manifesto in which he called for a European identity of harmonious coexistence and mutual fruition of Europe's great cultures. With this common European identity under threat at the time,

Military column on Julier Pass

Rolland articulated, from Geneva, what he considered to be the Swiss vocation:

> *I feel here how the generous heart of Switzerland is thrilled, divided between sympathies for the various nations, and lamenting that it cannot choose freely between them, nor even express them. I understand its torment; but I know that this is salutary. I hope it will rise thence to that superior joy of a harmony of races, which may be a noble example for the rest of Europe. It is the duty of Switzerland now to stand in the midst of the tempest, like an island of justice and of peace, where, as in the great monasteries of the early Middle Ages, the spirit may find a refuge from unbridled force; where the fainting swimmers of all nations, those who are weary of hatred, may persist, in spite of all the wrongs they have seen and suffered, in loving all men as their brothers.*

According to Rolland, Switzerland represented the last "island" on which this European identity could survive and thrive. Like "the great cloisters of the early Middle Ages", Switzerland was seen as a refuge for European pacifists like Rolland himself, but most especially for the very identity of Europe. Much as ancient knowledge had been saved from destruction because it had been preserved and recopied in cloisters – while barbarism outside cloister walls was destroying the continent – European identity and culture could be safeguarded in Switzerland, to be revived and flourish after conflict ended. Swiss neutrality was one reason for this confidence, but even more so was the country's shared culture with these two antagonistic nations, and soon three, when Italy entered the war the following year. What the Swiss experienced as a "divide" and "heartbreak" suggested their suitability and designation as this new European embodiment, and as such, protector of that identity.

A threatened "island": from "the Spirit of Munich" to "the Spirit of the Gotthard"

As we know, "the Spirit of Geneva" soon gave way to "the Spirit of Munich". Throughout the 1930s, Western democracies engaged in the politics of appeasement with Nazi Germany and Fascist Italy – essentially a form of capitulation not outrightly named as such. A growing coalition known as the "Axis" was forming, initially uniting Rome and Berlin, later with Moscow (1939), and finally, Tokyo (1940). Each of these nations, considering themselves enemies of the democracies, rearmed, annexed territories, and violated international conventions and peace treaties. Physically, Switzerland was situated at the core of the Rome-Berlin axis. In case of conflict, it risked being absorbed in joint action by the German army – soon augmented by the Austrian army – with that of Italy. Confronted with this threat, Switzerland started to prepare for arms – overtly, like France and England – with finances provided by the 1936 national military loan (an extraordinary war loan approved by the Swiss Federal Assembly to invest in needed armament). But, also like France and England, it had prepared too little, too late. Nonetheless, the Swiss political and military establishment had chosen their camp – with the democratic nations this time. Discussions with the French military command begun in 1936 led to a secret military alliance signed, for the Swiss, by General Henri Guisan in 1939.

In 1938, the Munich Agreement endorsed the *Anschluss* and the annexation of the Sudeten territory (in Czechoslovakia) by Germany. No one could ignore that war was imminent. It was also the year in which in Switzerland, the "Spirit of Geneva" finally ceded to the "Spirit of the Gotthard" or greater self-reliance. A declaration by Federal Councillor Philipp Etter (1891–1977) in 1938 sought to define Swiss identity and its indissoluble nature in "foreign" nations.

Before taking a closer look at Etter's declaration, a rarely noted fact is worth mentioning here. Like most European countries (France first and foremost), Switzerland in the 1930s was rife with antisemitism. In 1935, a Swiss edition of the *Protocols of the Elders of Zion* was distributed for pro-Nazi propaganda purposes at a demonstration in Bern organized by the far-right party National Front. The publication is a fraud, falsely purporting to prove the existence of an international Jewish plot aiming to destabilize nations and ensure universal domination for the Jewish people. It was said to have been written in Paris at the height of the Alfred Dreyfuss affair in 1895 by a collaborator of the Russian secret service to incite the Tsar to apply resolutely antisemitic policies. The Tsar was no dupe. Whatever its obscure origins, this grossly fraudulent account was nevertheless translated and widely distributed throughout all of Europe, fuelling the most radical discourse from Paris to Berlin. The notion of a "Jewish conspiracy", originating in the Middle Ages, had resurfaced in modern times and infiltrated the public conscience. Hitler himself based his "worldview" and his "battle" explicitly on this text. The Nuremberg Race Laws were conceived as Germany's response to this alleged "conspiracy".

In 1935, the year in which the Nuremberg Race Laws were enacted, the Swiss National Front brandished the text to influence Swiss public opinion and tip it into the pro-Nazi camp. It was a most turbulent time. The Jewish communities of Switzerland took the National Front to court for disseminating a "fraudulent" and "immoral" text. The judge in Bern hearing the case, Walter Meyer, admitted the "fraudulent" and "immoral" nature of the publication. This was the one time that the *Protocols of the Elders of Zion*, which had played such a critical role in the history of the twentieth century, was legally declared "fraudulent".

The Jewish communities' success was only partial, however: in 1937, a federal court revoked the designation of "immoral" on the grounds that it was a "political" text and refused to take any active measures against antisemitism. But the "fraudulent" nature of the text was not disputed. This incident is critical in the history of Switzerland because the refusal of the federal government to intervene directly propelled influential circles to take a stand and act as a result: men and women in the media, the army, political leadership, humanitarian circles and universities stood up against antisemitism, against Nazism and thereby against Germany. It was at this time that the secret alliance with France was initiated. This incident directly contributed to, or at least facilitated, the development of a spirit of resistance to Nazi Germany and led to Councillor Etter's declaration.

A spiritual identity:
"the Swiss idea" and the Gotthard Pass

In December 1938, three months after the Munich Agreement, Philipp Etter, the Federal Councillor from Zug responsible for the Federal Ministry of Home Affairs and Education, produced a remarkable document that laid out the principles of a national identity in no uncertain terms. Oddly enough, he presented this as a project rather than as a reality.

At a time of nationalist hysteria and unfettered rearmament, Etter considered it vital for Switzerland to engage the country in the promotion of "spiritual defence" (*Geistige Landesverteidigung*). The proposed measures implicated professional training facilities and schools, cultural activities, the arts, the media and a rapprochement of the country's linguistic components through a policy of systematic exchange.

In each of these domains, Etter advocated dynamic measures to reinforce the sentiment of belonging to a specific nation, which he considered to be no less important than the military measures under way to safeguard the "national community". As proof that such a sentiment of cohesion did not exist or insufficiently so, he asserted that the foremost cultural and linguistic components in Switzerland were allowing themselves to be beguiled by the dominant cultural influences on the other side of the country's borders, exposing Switzerland to a risk of implosion in case of conflict.

Etter defined the three core principles of Swiss identity in these terms:

1. Switzerland has its origins in three great Western civilizations and brings the three civilizations to co-inhabit on our territory
2. A federalist structure and the singular nature of Swiss democracy
3. Respect for human dignity and freedom.

The mentions of "democracy" and "respect for human dignity and freedom" may sound today like a provocation addressed to the Axis powers. Not so. Democracy has been at work in Switzerland since the Middle Ages, in some cantons. At least that was considered to be the case from the time that "national" historians had forged the myth of Swiss origins in the nineteenth century. What is certain is that in the Middle Ages a "free man" was neither a vassal nor a serf to anyone. Whereas he was a fairly rare occurrence in Europe in those times when feudal ties governed a good portion of society, in fact the entire population in the valleys of Central Switzerland enjoyed this status already at that time. As for bringing "the three great Western civilizations" to co-inhabit "on our territory", that is obvious, if we set aside the fact that in place of Switzerland's three languages Etter substitutes a broader cultural heritage.

The Gotthard symbol:
representing a "spirit", not a "race"

Indeed, for Etter, "the Gotthard" – "source of the Rhine, Rhône and Ticino rivers" – both "divides and unites these three cultural regions, the most important in Western history". It is, indeed, precisely "around the Gotthard range", which "simultaneously divides and unites" the country, that Swiss statehood was born. In 1938, while the country's political reality was unquestionable, its cultural identity was far from certain, constituted as it was on the premise of an "ideal" instead of on a reality in the sense that the "essence and mission" of the "federal state" that was established around the Gotthard range and the Gotthard Pass were designated "spiritual" rather than political in nature. The French, German and Italian cultures, which were both separated and united by Switzerland, had developed within this country's borders more "purely", having been spared the torments of exclusive nationalism that had infected these countries in 1938.

When in Italy, Germany and even France, culture was subordinated to the nation and racial theories would soon provoke the horrors that followed, Switzerland was spared this fate by its very essence: "We refuse to accept a theory according to which the State and its borders are determined on the basis of race". How could it possibly be otherwise in a tripartite cultural environment sharing the same political territory? If "one people" and hence one language and one culture were the determining factors of a state or "an empire" – this triad recalling the grim Nazi-party slogan – then Switzerland was destined to disappear. In this respect, only a centripetal force could counter the centrifugal nationalist thrust, to exist as a nation but also, moreover, to nurture that highest of human ideals: "The Swiss idea (or *raison d'être*) is not founded on race or, in other words, it is not a work of the flesh but rather a work of the spirit". Nothing is so strong and yet at the same time so vulnerable as a "work of the spirit". Since this "idea" is of a "spiritual" essence, the implication is that it must be believed in and that the forces of reason must be solicited in its defence against any natural penchant towards agitation on linguistic or cultural grounds. Even today, the significance of this rejection of the notion of "race" – in terms of a foundational requisite determining the identity of a "people" – is not fully measured. Contrary to the ideal of a country like republican France, for example, Swiss "national" cohesion can never be achieved by language, by culture or by a centralized state.

Switzerland sees itself as a crossroads nation at the heart of which three great continental cultures flourish harmoniously in a free and democratic space. Beyond ensuring peaceful coexistence, the democratic state was to guarantee the "mutual enrichment" of the cultures at a time when everything colluded to pitting them against one other.

The only identity that Switzerland apparently wishes to espouse is the universalist ideal conveyed by Romain Rolland. At least this is what Councillor Etter asserted in 1938. Switzerland is an "idea" that is destined to materialize through the interpenetration of European cultures in a democratic and peaceful environment. This is what the Gotthard symbolizes. Attaining this ideal would be "a victory of mind over matter" at a time when the tide of history seemed to annihilate the forces of reason and reduce men to the recesses of their most brutal instincts.

The Gotthard and its passes take on a doubly symbolic dimension: they are at one and the same time the crossroads of the "three most important cultures" and a place of passage from one world to another, and a partitioning and confinement in troubled times, the last refuge of an "idea" that is utterly crucial because it is universal and not the bastion of a "race" that rises up against others.

Six roads and six passes cut across the Gotthard, each of which links the four cardinal directions, and the four major political forces on the continent that surrounded Switzerland in 1918: the Austro-Hungarian Empire, the German Reich, Italy and France. But above all, this communication node links the four linguistic regions in the country. Furka links Valais and Uri; Oberalp links Grisons and Uri, Susten links Bern and Uri; the Göschenen road links the Swiss Plateau with the Andermatt crossroads and thus with Valais, with Grisons and Ticino. Finally, the Gotthard itself, situated at the mouth of the Andermatt basin, links all of these roads with the canton of Ticino. And insofar as the notion of "the Gotthard range" is extended that distance, Nüffenen, which borders the Gotthard on the southwest slope, links Valais and beyond it the Lake Geneva region directly to Ticino. As the epicentre of the passes, the Gotthard is first and foremost an ensemble of domestic passages. The international border is located nearly 100 km to the south at Chiasso, which opens the way to the plains of Lombardy (Italy). No national border divides the Gotthard range, which remains continuously open to free passage from one canton to another, weather permitting. The Gotthard is thus doubly significant: it epitomizes the various components of the national identity, which is itself embedded in a continental European culture that defines the *raison d'être* of that identity.

Etter's stroke of genius – specifically addressed to the Swiss and not to the Germans or Italians – was to have harmonized, for the first time ever, all the components of Swiss identity on the basis of a geographic reality, namely the Gotthard range and an ensemble of Alpine passes of utmost strategic importance. History – as unpredictable as it is – would prove him right.

The collapse of Europe and fortification of the Alps ("National Reduit")

The French and English military disaster in the spring of 1940 put Switzerland in an awkward position. No one could have foreseen that these two nations, victorious in 1918, would see their operations utterly destroyed in a three-week military campaign that stunned the world. It would take two years to overcome the stupor into which the *Blitzkrieg* had plunged them; the English were saved by their insular context and the Russians owed their salvation to the 2,000 kilometres that separate Moscow from the Vistula.

The Swiss army had sided with London and Paris to the point of concluding a secret military alliance with them. In May 1940, Defensive Counter Air operations and Swiss fighter planes shot down eleven German aircraft that had violated Swiss airspace, flying over the Plateau in an attempt to reach France. Officially, the action was one way of defending Swiss neutrality. Unofficially, it was also a signal to the English and French that the southern flank of the Allied forces was secure. The Swiss would not flinch.

The Germans didn't leave it at that: Hitler was enraged over the episode and personally took charge of the aftermath, demanding explanations, apologies, guarantees, compensation and repatriation of the Luftwaffe pilots. The German pilots suffered additional humiliation upon learning that not only had they been shot down by Swiss anti-aircraft cannons but also by the latest Messerschmitt Bf 109 planes, bearing the Swiss Federal Cross. This proved that, at equivalent weapon calibre, Swiss pilots could win over the experienced Germans despite the combat training of the latter acquired during the three years they had sided with Franco in Spain.

The army and the Swiss population were jubilant, nearly as much although more discreetly, as during the legendary match at the World Soccer Cup quarter-final in Paris in 1938 when the Swiss team beat the "Reich's" team 4 to 2. Three weeks later, these victories would be a source of embarrassment for the Swiss: in occupied Paris, German intelligence officers found documents confirming the secret alliance between France and Switzerland. The day after French capitulation on 23 June 1940, Hitler ordered that a plan be developed "to take Switzerland by surprise" and posted the 12th Army commanded by Field Marshall Wilhelm List along the length of the Jura border in France. Operation Tannenbaum presumed that the Swiss Plateau could be taken within three days.

Mussolini's armies were to take the Alps, but no time-frame had been specified for that operation. It was the great unknown in this plan.

Intelligence services in Bern got wind of these intentions owing to efficient connections to Berlin. On 24 June, the president of the Swiss Confederation Marcel Pilet-Golaz made a highly ambiguous statement advocating authoritarian restoration of democracy – all too reminiscent of the State re-establishment advocated by Maréchal Pétain on the other side of the Jura mountains. It appeared that Bern was capitulating without even having taken up arms. Active collaboration with Germany appeared imminent, even more so since in Bern, Pilet-Golaz had warmly welcomed representatives of the Swiss National Front which supported alignment with the Axis powers.

But at the same time, in a double-barrelled approach characteristic of Swiss policy in times of crisis, the chief of the Swiss military command General Henri Guisan was given free rein to reorganize the front in response to this new situation. Colonel Oscar Adolf Germann (a real if surprising name) advocated a retreat of the majority of troops to the "National Reduit", or Alpine fortifications. This was not a new defence strategy. It was first introduced when Switzerland became a neutral state in 1815 following the Congress of Vienna. The strategy involved securing all the points of crossing over the Alps, including all the Alpine passes, and closing them to enemy troops by making the routes impracticable and too onerous to use. The time had come for its first large-scale implementation.

General Guisan chose this option, the only one possible, but left some troops stationed on the Plateau and at official border crossings to slow the enemy down and reassure the population. He was not a brilliant strategist nor the architect of an ingenious course of action, but he was most certainly a brilliant communicator and a man of unwavering will. While Pilet-Golaz was ostensibly paving the way for collaboration with the enemy, stoking his rhetoric with Pétainist references, Guisan adopted a posture and tone resembling de Gaulle's celebrated address, the "Appeal of 18 June". On 25 July 1940, Guisan brought the 450 commanding officers of the Swiss army to the symbolic Rütli Meadow at the foot of the Gotthard where he invoked resistant spirit, courage and combat. He made sure that his official statement, with generous margin for improvisation during delivery, was widely shared with the population in both print and image. In the circumstances, the message was also addressed to the Germans, undoubtedly relayed to Berlin by their diplomatic and intelligence services.

The Rütli is the symbolic heart of Switzerland: the myth or legend surrounding it – whose degree of truth no one really knows – holds that representatives of the cantons of Uri, Schwyz and Nidwalden met secretly at Rütli in 1291 to form an alliance against Austrian invaders. This secret meeting is credited with providing the conditions for the great victory of the three cantons over the Austrians at Morgarten in 1315, which subsequently led to the official pact establishing a "confederacy" of sovereign states.

General Guisan solicited the national and combative sentiment of a people severely fractured by the preceding conflict, a people that had not fought side-by-side for centuries. His address appeared naïve at first. It is as though the general had imagined that the enchantment and scene-setting at the mythical Rütli site could in and of itself heal the shortfall of national sentiment that Federal Councillor Etter had highlighted two years earlier.

On the contrary, Guisan's strategy seemed perfectly attuned to reality. First, the Swiss had participated in all the European conflicts since the Middle Ages, be it in entire regiments of mercenaries or in isolated groups, as during the Spanish Civil War. Second, the "Alpine Reduit" strategy could only succeed in operational terms: the goal was to resist as long as possible on the best defensive terrain imaginable, destroying all access points to it, as needed. Third, the "Alpine Reduit" was only one component of a larger global strategy that also included diplomatic and economic action. Switzerland having committed to the transit of trading goods through its territory by virtue of its neutrality, the Nazis would have no advantage whatsoever in invading Switzerland only to then have to restore hundreds of bridges, tunnels and access roads to the passes. The strategic axis connecting the "Reich" with the Mediterranean Sea was maintained (and sustained) by the Swiss, in exchange for their freedom. Moreover, Switzerland's independence guaranteed the Nazi government the option of buying the Swiss francs it needed for trade with other neutral countries and to buy the raw materials so essential to feeding their war effort: fuel, rubber, steel, etc.

Switzerland had offered the Allies the same guarantees, but they did not avail of them, or hardly, as Switzerland was surrounded by Reich-controlled territories. It soon became challenging to deliver to England the famous Oerlikon cannons the English had ordered in massive numbers. Following the disastrous incident in June 1940, production plans for the cannon were secretly dispatched off to London where, with the consent of the Swiss federal authorities, the Swiss company licensed its manufacture to England. The Allies built a far greater number of these cannons during the hostilities than the Swiss themselves could ever have managed to produce. But from the outset, the geographic location of their construction presented an asymmetry in the (official) application of the principal of neutrality, which reflected badly on Switzerland's reputation after the war. This is a complex issue. We know since the end of the twentieth century that certain government practices and dealings of Swiss business leaders were compromising, and even remiss on moral grounds in some cases. But for the Swiss population in general, who did not benefit from these dealings, the war was a long ordeal.

The Alpine passes were the linchpin of the Reduit strategy. Closed and tightly guarded as no pass had ever been before, Switzerland had mined the railway tunnels under the passes but left their core open to potential enemy passage, which the Swiss were preparing day and night to repel at the surface.

The fortifications capped three major axes: the Gotthard, Simplon and Great St Bernard Passes, extending nearly 70 kilometres for the latter. From Fort Chillon on the shore of Lake Geneva stretching through to the eastern border with Austria, the entire Alpine region or nearly one-third of the country's surface had become a strategic military zone where everything was subordinated to the military imperative (see map 8, p. 244).

Inside, the fortification installations were impressive. To anyone who has visited the since-decommissioned sites, they were clearly designed to serve: equipped with field hospital operating rooms, mess halls, showers, recreation areas and, especially, indirect-fire shooting posts. This ingenious, purely mechanical system allows firing at a target that cannot be seen by the aimer, guided by spotters hidden in towers camouflaged as rock: a plan imitates the entire range of the shooting angle on which a target moves as the firearm is used.

Life revolved around a weekly protocol indicating the passage of time, not otherwise felt inside: included were sunrise and sunset (times), not seen from the inside, or just barely (through a telescopic lens); the outside temperature (not otherwise felt); the degree of sunshine (merely a word, or at best a drawing on paper), and so on. In the mountain's hard-rock bosom soldiers were strangely isolated from the land they were defending, "interred" or "immured" for weeks at a time, ever watchful for the would-be aggressor. In the event he finally arrived, the pass would have to be defended on both slopes and to the bitter end, "with no mind for retreat", as General Guisan had instructed. Retreat to where? The plan was to hold out long enough to physically destroy all the access points to the pass, at the risk of being buried alive. This gave rise to unprecedented symptoms in the half-terrified soldiers there, while on the Plateau down below families continued to live a relatively normal life, unawares. And yet, in the event of an attack, it was the civilians below who were most exposed to any reprisals by an enemy made anxious by the resistance at the passes.

The nature of the pass had changed. Transformed into the opposite of what it had always been, the pass was closed, partitioned and, paradoxically, itself required defence. To the soldiers guarding it, the pass came to represent the entire nation, albeit reduced to the small plateau at the summit, where nothing could grow in a ground covered by snow seven months of the year. The only semblance of life there were excessively armed soldiers with whom to exchange a password.

As a strategy, opening the tunnels and closing the Alpine passes drew criticism somewhat later. How odd, it seemed at first, to expose civilians to the enemy in the flatlands below while tucking soldiers away in the cavities of Alpine bedrock. But it worked. Switzerland was not invaded and did not have to take up arms. It thus avoided active collaboration with the Nazis, to which virtually all the occupied governments were forced to consent. Perhaps the plan's most enduring success was to have made Councillor Etter's dream of national cohesion become a reality in only a short time.

The exterior threat (a very real one for anyone in uniform), the frightened population, and the restrictions and requirements of such peculiar armed service at long last motivated a national sentiment. Even today it is embodied in the Gotthard, which was both the heart of the Reduit operation and at the same time the most frequented commercial train route for the entire duration of the war. It remains the symbol of the Swiss resistance that ultimately shaped the nation, for the first time ever, during the six years of the Second World War.

Battle for the tunnels

The second half of the twentieth century completed the process by which Alpine passes lost their strategic significance to the Alpine tunnels. The passes transformed into playgrounds and memorial sites, while history was unfolding underneath the mountains faster than ever.

Inaugurated in 1964, the Great St Bernard road tunnel was the first to service year-round passage through the Alps. Opening of the Gotthard road tunnel followed sixteen years later, in 1980, becoming – as was already customary in the Alps – the world's longest road tunnel (16.9 kilometres). A second tube slated to double the tunnel surface is expected in 2029.

The Gotthard Base Tunnel has been in operation since 2016. At 57 kilometres, it is the world's longest and deepest railway tunnel, making the Gotthard a record winner once again, in all categories.

The story of this tunnel is worth mentioning because it is illustrative of Switzerland's place in Europe and of the Gotthard's place in Switzerland.

Beginning at the end of the 1940s, Western Europe opened to commercial exchange in an unprecedented manner, going as far as to unite into one European Economic Community (EEC) in 1957. Looking westward to North America and eastward to Asia via, respectively, the Atlantic Ocean and the Mediterranean Sea, Europe saw Switzerland as the point of intersection between these two geographic poles. And indeed, the country lies along the route linking Rotterdam, Antwerp and Hamburg with Genoa. The second Gotthard railway tunnel project was launched in 1947. The first, in 1881, obliged trains to climb access ramps on both sides at slow speed and was not robust enough to sustain the exponential traffic increase that was anticipated at the beginning of *les Trente Glorieuses* (the thirty-year period of economic growth in Europe in the post-war years 1945–1975). It was decided that a base tunnel was needed for bi-directional rail traffic through the Alps at speeds of more than 200 kilometres per hour.

Therein began a long and complex process that was clinched as of 1992, when a Swiss popular referendum endorsed construction of the Gotthard Base Tunnel. The repercussions of this extended far beyond Swiss borders. Europe at the start of the 1990s was very keen on road travel. A network of motorways was built across the continent, from Hamburg to Cádiz, whereas the rail tunnels involved offloading at some point and were not a straight run.

On this subject, there is an amusing story in Switzerland that is less well known abroad. Before an assembly of European transport ministers who were advocating building motorways in the Alps and passage through them via road tunnels, Adolf Ogi, then Federal Councillor of the Ministry of Transport, defended instead a double-rail transversal project involving the Lötschberg-Simplon and the Gotthard. The European proposal meant that Alpine valleys would be sacrificed by the construction of the additional infrastructure needed and the Plateau region would suffocate under the weight of the 40-ton trucks crisscrossing Europe via Switzerland.

A pragmatist, Adolf Ogi succeeded in convincing the ministers by taking them on a site visit, by helicopter, so they could see for themselves why it would be impossible to build motorways at the designated locations which were beneath the church at Wassen, on the Gotthard axis, and then on the Lötschberg ascent. As the story goes, the helicopter pilot administered a series of in-flight "jolts" for the visiting Belgian minister, at Adolf Ogi's request. According to Minister Ogi, it was fear that had incited the minister to change his mind… But more likely, even before those memorable jolts, the day had been won by the spectacular sight of the dizzying slopes around the Lötschberg valley, as immaculate as they were unsuitable for a four-lane motorway by the very nature of their topography. What's more, no practicable roadway had ever crossed the Lötschberg Pass, melding as it does with the vertigo-inducing acclivities, when descended on foot, from the Gemmi on the Valais side. Adolf Ogi's compatriots admire in him a twenty-first-century version of the mythical William Tell. No Gotthard muleteer, Ogi was a ski instructor from Kandersteg. Without a crossbow but armed with an everlasting smile and an instinctive intelligence all his own, Ogi single-handedly opposed the steamroller of European diplomacy. In both the William Tell and Adolf Ogi stories, David had conquered Goliath over Alpine passage. Yet again, the passes played a decisive role in the destiny of Switzerland.

That same year, 1992, the Swiss refused to join the European Union, mustering the wherewithal, once again, to remain faithful to the country's paradoxical vocation as a transit corridor that ensures, at its own expense, the construction and maintenance of infrastructure that provides the European continent with the vital passageways that it needs. Switzerland nevertheless remains a resolutely independent country, capable of steadfastly holding forth against mightier adversaries, winning the upper hand with artful persuasion.

The Gotthard Base Tunnel was built and later duplicated at Lötschberg, where construction also began in 1994 and a second tube is slated to open in 2030. A rail speed record of 280 kilometres per hour was surpassed in the first Lötschberg tunnel in 2006. Switzerland is largely ahead of its neighbours France, Italy and Austria in implementing the European high-speed transalpine rail programme. In fact, as the only country to have implemented it to date, Switzerland is ensured of a quasi-monopoly on the Northern Europe–Mediterranean axis.

At the top of the Gotthard today is a gleaming replica of the legendary horse-drawn postal coach that ran along the Tremola road in the nineteenth century, its bells and coachman's horn jingling and swaying with the coach around the sharp turns. Two thousand metres below, it takes passenger trains a mere two hours and forty minutes to link Zurich with Milan.

Memorial site

Cyclists, camping vehicles, local buses, motorcycles and cars of all makes climb their way to the top of the Gotthard to park at the foot of the hospice and in front of the Gotthard Museum. Fifty metres higher, the imposing remnants of the decommissioned fortifications sit at the start of the Tremola road opposite the Chapel of the Dead where tribute used to be paid to the memory of "wayfarers" who had died of the cold or exhaustion. Today, a high-voltage power line streaks through the western horizon and the blades of wind turbines whistle in the air. Here, a thousand years of history clash within a mere few hectares.

Close observation of the visitors on the small plateau at the top of the Gotthard indicates that they all appear to follow the same ritual, albeit in variable order: they take in a view of the lake, stop at the sausage stand, some climb up to the fortifications, have coffee, visit the museum, the church (though not many go there) and the hospice. And between these various "stations", there is inevitably an incredulous gaze at the horizon. "Here we are, on the Gotthard." One thousand years of history, the soul of a nation, the heart of Europe. This modern-day ritual is captured in a dozen or so photos taken with a cell phone. And by then, it's time to go! An average of thirty minutes at the top is usually enough before it's time to descend back to "life" below, our version of it, the same way we went up: without much effort (even for the cyclists). On bright and sunny days, the din of vehicle engines can be deafening. Should fog or a storm surprise these modern-day pilgrims they are reminded that the frightful mountain is still there, as unpredictable and dangerous as ever, and that it is completely oblivious to man, however much we may believe that we have mastered it.

The Gotthard apocalypse

Above Andermatt, at the intersection of the two Alpine rail links, hectares of canvas are stretched tautly every spring to contain the melting of the Gemstock glacier and preserve the village's ski slopes. The initiative has both amused and irritated glaciologists. "Putting a cast on a wooden leg!" accused one in 2005, according to the Swiss French-language newspaper *Le Temps*. Instead, it would make more sense to tackle the human causes of climate change.

Their consequences are measurable and clear. One European scientific programme in which Switzerland participates studies the effects of permafrost melting in Europe. Universities in Switzerland and Germany are focusing on the Gotthard range. Samples of previously frozen earth, untouched for thousands of years, were analysed by researchers for their bacteria content – bacteria that heat will eventually reactivate and free. What would happen if these bacteria, many of which are unknown to us, proved dangerous for animal life and hence for us? The melting of Alpine glaciers each year deposits increasing amounts of these bacteria into rivers, and notably the famous "four rivers that irrigate Europe: the Rhine, Rhône, Reuss and Ticino", to quote Etter who, when he uttered those words in 1938, was far from imagining that the Alpine rivers could be anything but life-giving.

THE PASS AS A SOURCE OF SPIRITUALITY

Frédéric Möri

Tschingelhörner, seen from Segnes Pass

A spiritual place: the "port"

A spiritual place is a nodal point where the real and the imaginary intersect. People tend to give it a particular aura and meaning: the source, the cave, the port, the summit, the way, etc. The more that frequenting such a place implies some kind of break with the ordinary course of existence, the stronger the articulation between the real and the imaginary will be. And the more regularly it is frequented, and essential to life, the more it will acquire an autonomous symbolic dimension: passing through a tunnel, revitalizing, the path of life, and so on.

Thus the seaport, where for ages people were compelled or even forced to pass through, came to symbolize passage into the next life if it was the point of departure, or conversely, a place of rest and salvation if you arrived there after an uncertain sea crossing. Similarly, taking a difficult path, infested with brigands, exposing the traveller to fatigue and illness yet also to foundational experience took on a broader significance as the image of the man on the way or on a quest, *homo viator, peregrinus*. It became the symbol of the human condition, imposing on us all a perilous journey from birth to death.

The French word *col* simply refers to an indentation in mountainous relief. It says nothing about what crossing the pass was like for the men who did so over the millennia. The German term *Pass* offers a broader meaning. As we have seen, it is both a "narrow and difficult passage, notably from one country to another", but also "an invitation to continue one's journey freely". The Romans called it *portus* in the sense of opening or passage, but also (sea)port, asylum and refuge. The names of some passes still evoke this original meaning: the Somport, Port, Portet and Pourtalet passes in the Pyrenees. Most of these passes still feature the foundations of the hospitable facilities and sanctuaries built there in the Middle Ages. At the major Alpine passes in Switzerland, such facilities are still operational at the Gotthard, the Great St Bernard and the Simplon Passes.

In the broadest geographical sense, *portus* includes the routes leading up to and down from the passes; water springs – in abundance – at which people and beasts refresh and find the energy to cross the passes; the summits towering over access routes, particularly terrifying when no one had trod there previously; rivers, followed up to the final ramps; the ascent, by dint of calf muscle; passage itself, from one slope to another, and thereby from one reality to another; the tunnel – the oldest dating from the eighteenth century – and finally, safe haven, nestling at the summit, flanked by a sanctuary dedicated to the mountain god: Penn for the Celts, Jupiter for the Romans, then Yahweh-God for Christianized peoples. The sanctuary offered travellers peace of mind by ritually warding off the ever-present dangers along the way.

Thinking about it, the whole thing is almost unique in terms of symbolic and spiritual charge. Provided you surrender yourself body and soul to the venture by the strength of your legs, rather than ducking out of the effort in an engine-powered vehicle. Today, the pass can be crossed in an hour or two, from one valley to the next, in the comfortable, air-conditioned safety of a car. It is no longer necessary to truly cross over or surmount anything. Travellers pass by, or are effortlessly carried across the pass in a mechanically built temporal and spatial artifice, without any real contact with the elements. Motor-aided passage today has done away with the spiritual dimension of Alpine passage by eliminating our direct confrontation with the physical and psychological limitations of our existence. Sports enthusiasts or adventure-seeking hikers may still find Alpine passes challenging to cross, but their experience is far removed in both nature and intensity from what has been the essence of that experience in the Alps for nearly 2,000 years.

For travellers before our time, crossing a pass involved a three- or four-day journey at least. Those undertaking Alpine passage could temporarily feel like a *peregrinus,* far more than was possible on the plains below: a man on a journey, with no homeland, at once surrendering to the force of the elements and receptive to the beauty of the world. The alchemy of the various symbolic components that punctuated "passage" could then come into play, liberating and nourishing the traveller's imagination and introspection, over and above any fatigue and fear he may have felt.

This symbolic confrontation was extremely fertile for almost two millennia, until the end of the nineteenth century, when the "port" became the "pass" with the development of carriageways and then mechanization. It is this spiritual dimension, which today's tourists sometimes still seek more or less consciously but rarely find, that we wish to evoke now.

Terror

As we have seen, from the time of the Roman expansion into transalpine Gaul, the Great St Bernard Pass became the main thoroughfare enabling the development of Roman power in the West. In the first century AD, the Latin poet Silius Italicus (26–101) gives a largely romanticized account of the crossing of the Alps by the armies of Hannibal Barca three centuries earlier. In the third century BC, Carthage and the Roman Republic were locked in a duel to the death for control of the Mediterranean and its commercial prospects. Hannibal, one of the best strategists of Antiquity, was the first to understand the importance of this route, which was considered impassable by an army on campaign. He decided to use it in winter to turn the entire Roman army on its head.

Silius' testimony is of limited historical reliability: it has been known since Antiquity that it is not certain that Hannibal and his troops crossed the Alps at the Great St Bernard location. But we do know that they did cross the Alps somewhere. Be that as it may, Silius' text is invaluable because it helps us to understand what a major pass could have been like for people in the early years of our era. Silius constructs a representation that had certainly prevailed since time immemorial and that would continue to do so until the sixteenth century. For us, his account represents the starting point of the pass experience.

The pass is the point at which passage is possible and necessary, but it is also a place of terror and death, where man is confronted with the brute force of the elements, considered to be supernatural. This anxiety that men felt before nature, expressed in constant references to mythology, is indeed born of man's confrontation with real geography, of which we can still identify – more or less – the main components.

The first element highlighted by Silius is the conjunction of the escarpment of the "mountain flanks", through which passage leads, and the "age-old ice" towering over them.

We know that the average temperature at that time was lower than it is today, only slightly lower than it was at the time of the "Little Ice Age" (fourteenth to sixteenth centuries), and the peaks that frame the Great St Bernard Pass, for example, are nearly at an altitude of 3,000 metres. It is not implausible to compare the experience of the last ramps up to the pass with braving an "eternal winter".

The summer sun was unable to melt the ice that covered the peaks, which was astonishing to men from the plains. And when the snow on the slopes did begin to melt in spring, it was only to swallow the travellers whole. Storms, crevasses and avalanches, all clearly mentioned in the text, were very real scourges for men who did not have the option of tunnels and could not afford to wait for fine weather to pass through.

The pass is thus presented by Silius as a non-place in terms of the space-time dimension of men: excluded from the beneficial alternation of the seasons, it immerses the traveller in a universe characterized by excess. Indeed, nothing here is on a human scale. Not the terrain, not the wind, not the slippery ground, not even the people who live permanently on the slopes of the massif and seem to belong to another world: "half-savage", their "hideous heads bristling with icicles", the natives haunt these unlikely places like spectres or damned souls, appearing from nowhere to torment, rob or murder travellers. Hannibal's army, although formidable, also had to contend with them, according to Roman historians.

For the man of that time, inhabited by the mythologies that were his own, such passage was akin to a real crossing of the Underworld. Hell, for the Romans, was made of ice and darkness. "This abyss in the realm of pale shadows", this "Styx", the river of the Underworld, to which the road is compared, is perhaps the Combe des Morts at the bottom of which one ventured, making one's way alongside the torrent, in the shadow of what would later be known as Mont Mort and Grande Chenalette, exposed to the mercy of avalanches and terrible gusts of wind. It is hardly surprising, therefore, that contemporaries believed that only Hercules could have opened the door to this way. If the real "Tartarus", where the "Styx" flows, is a subterranean hell, writes Silius, the elevation of the massif is its mirror image, a hell of altitude where the light of the sky is hidden beneath the disproportionate shadows of the peaks and the veil of inclement weather. An abyss under open sky that people can cross while still alive, at the exact junction of the habitable world and the realm of the Beyond.

Silius' text is first and foremost an exercise in style, a literary "topos" known as a *locus terribilis*. It consists of making a place, by dint of hyperbole and parallels with imaginary places (in this case, with the Underworld), one of absolute horror, from which nothing can save us. It is the poet's way of striking his reader's spirit. It is also a way for the historian to emphasize the qualities and value of those who defy such a place, pass through

Passengers in an open-top postal bus

Man travelling alone on a mountain road

it and return to tell the tale (in this case Hannibal); finally, for the propagandist of the Roman Empire, it was a thinly veiled means of glorifying the greatness of those who would eventually tame it, to one degree or another. At the time of Silius' writing, the Roman power had just definitively opened the way and made it into a real port. By crowning the highest crossing in the Alps at the time with a sanctuary dedicated to Jupiter, god of Rome, and equipping it with a wide carriageway, the Empire symbolically appropriated a place that until then, as Silius reminded us, had escaped human control almost completely. It symbolizes man's mastery over the elements.

The pass, and this one in particular, has been a highly spiritual place since ancient times. Men having been obliged to cross here, the human experience of that passage was such that it became almost natural for the poet to make it the junction of human and divine realities, of life and death, of the natural and supranatural. A fact all the more remarkable in that, becoming a port, or opening, it became one of the most crucial locations for the development of the world's first empire.

Along with the desert and the ocean, the pass is a border with blurred contours, beyond which reality changes in nature. The returning traveller will for a long time populate his account with supernatural figures, in his attempt to convey the stupor or horror that seized him during passage. The desert and the ocean marked the periphery of the world known to ancient Europeans. Sight of land was never lost for long when navigating the seas, and the real desert – the one requiring forty days for crossing without sight of any water source – existed only in the tales of the "black men" with whom trade was conducted in the trading posts of Proconsular Africa or Syria. The Alpine pass, however, was central, located as it was at the very heart of the vital living space of the peoples of Europe since the dawn of man, at the exact point of junction, or nearly so, of the four cardinal points of the Roman Empire. For the traveller, it remained a "terrible place" until at least the sixteenth century, by which time horror had taken on a new meaning, alongside wonder.

Eschatology

Zurich humanist Josias Simler (1530–1576) authored one of the first works of Swiss political history, *La République helvétique*, and the first work dedicated to the Alps, *De Alpibus Commentarius* (1574). It proposes "a first attempt at a comprehensive understanding of the Alps, in space and in time" and "a first encyclopaedic guide", says Claude Reichler in his anthology, *Le Voyage en Suisse* (1998).

As a good humanist, Simler bases his writing on the ancient authors, who were then the ultimate reference for all modern thinking. He published a large excerpt from the *Punica* by Silius Italicus, a seminal text that he considered to be still relevant in his time, and supplemented it with accounts by Jovius (1483–1552), a modern author, describing the Gotthard Pass in detail. This modern perspective corresponded to that of Silius at a time when the Gotthard was gaining in importance.

Horror struck intrepid travellers who were obliged to cross the Gotthard in unfavourable seasonal conditions, just as it did the Carthaginian soldier at the Great St Bernard Pass. On the Ticino side, the Tremolo Bridge, literally "the bridge that trembles", does not itself tremble, says the author: it is the travellers who shake with terror as they cross it. On the other flank, the names of the valley and the bridge over the Reuss also belong to the world of the damned: "Höllschlucht" (Valley of Hell), "Teufelsbrücke" (Devil's Bridge). These two harrowing features that frame the dark massif, which for a long time was considered – wrongly – to be the highest in Europe, impose a two-fold ordeal: passage is terrible in both directions. Between these two focal points of horror were avalanches, precipices, and vertiginous paths, at times cut into the rock such as at Twärren Bridge. The challenge of vertigo and the horror of being submerged beneath the torrents of snow and ice that are said to pour down upon the road at the slightest sound made by the traveller were two antagonistic torments inflicted on the reckless merchants and smugglers of Uri and Airolo. Their distant heirs would make the Gotthard the heart of Europe's great transversal network, but at the end of the Middle Ages, it was far from being the most important crossroads in Europe. And as Simler reminds us, death was frequent. The infernal analogy is not just a metaphor.

With Simler's account, in printed form, the black legend of the Gotthard responds to the ancient vision of the Great St Bernard by Silius. The two passes, placed as if in mirror image in this vast work, mark the two poles of the Swiss Alps.

Paradoxically, in our view, it is precisely at the highest point of passage that refuge, safety and rest can be found temporarily. Simler scarcely mentions this, but the Gotthard – like the Great St Bernard – is well worth a visit. As a "port" it offers a hospice and a sanctuary, where prayers were not merely a matter of form, or even the privilege of passing travellers: for centuries, the chapel drew a major regional pilgrimage. From spring to autumn, inhabitants from the five surrounding valleys made their way up in procession on fixed dates to venerate Saint Gotthard, Bishop of Mainz, a tireless evangelist and above all a healer: the man of God has the power to neutralize the excessive force of the elements from God himself. As early as 1230, only a short time after the major works that were carried out by the Walser, an altar was dedicated to Saint Gotthard at the summit of the pass. Like a new Hercules, Gotthard symbolically opened the way and was, in those times when the invisible world was omnipresent, the heart of the efforts that enabled a sense of security along the way.

In the thirteenth century, the countryside and towns were dotted with a dense network of calvaries, chapels and votive altars. There was not a single crossroads nor junction – not even a secondary one – that was not stamped with the seal of God, guaranteeing his presence. No one would ever have ventured on this new way regularly without the benefit of this spiritual sustenance.

As with the Great St Bernard, and during the same period, the pilgrimage to the Gotthard became a self-imposed challenge, almost gratuitously. The phenomenon was not marginal: in his *Cosmographie universelle*, published in 1544, Sébastian Münster (1488–1552) referred to the 600 or so travellers who were accommodated in the Great Saint-Bernard Hospice every night as "pilgrims" (*peregrini*). In the Middle Ages, the word pilgrims referred first and foremost to those who set out on the way to a major shrine at great risk to their life. But there were so many pilgrims on the roads that they came to be equated with travellers. Be that as it may, the large number of people who visited the pass in all seasons speaks highly of the vitality of the Alpine sanctuary and the utility of the infrastructure that was maintained there at great cost.

The singular geography of the area took on a different meaning for those who tackled the pass out of devotion: it was seen as a crossing of the underworld where each person could read, as if inscribed in the cursed topography, an allegorical itinerary. Taking the example of the Gotthard, the elevation and the ascent, of course, are those of the soul towards the eternal light; the Devil's Bridge is the "narrow way", the only possible way, over the abyss; the narrow path cut into the flanks of the rocky ridge is "the way and the life" – there is no other way. Dominated by the immense granite barrier overlooking the waters of the Reuss raging in springtime, pilgrims could feel the words of the psalm in their very being: "Though I walk through the valley of the shadow of death I will fear no evil, for thou art with me" (Ps. 23:4).

Once past the plateau linking Andermatt to Hospental, the ascent begins again: 400 metres of acclivity by leg power, steep at first, then gently sloping across the vastness of the Gamsteg plain. At the foot of a massive ridge, the path runs alongside the Reuss river, revealing an awe-inspiring landscape. To the left – for those coming from the north – is "the mountain, as if it were part of another world", to quote Simler. You don't climb it, but walk alongside it for almost an hour through a coomb of russet grass. For the pilgrims of the time, this "other world" was a real treasure, recalling the significance of the Sinai. At the foot of the inviolate sanctuary of Adonai, "God of the mountain", the declivity and the murmur of the waters offered respite, and time to meditate on the words of the prophet: "Where were you when I laid the foundations of the earth?" (Job, 38:4).

Higher up still, past the last ramps, you cross a desolate landscape, essentially mineral and monochrome, inhospitable to living creatures. The path seeks a way through the heaps of cyclopean rock, in what is, strictly speaking, the Gotthard Pass. Here, the "Devil" no longer comes to do his frightening work, but death itself is present, it seems, when the heavens open. Here, man was long reminded of the precariousness of his condition. In the passage itself, the "chapel of the Dead" was built as a kind of supplication, slightly away from the Hospice, as at the Great Saint-Bernard. It overlooks the "lago dei Morti". The road then winds its way along the "Ri di Fortunei" to the foot of the summits known as "Alpe di Fortunei", which run along the southern slopes of the massif, before crossing the torrent on the "Bridge of Ashes". The ancient goddess of Fortune, and equally her heir, the medieval allegory of Destiny, are fundamentally ambivalent. Man, who is forever Destiny's pawn, according to the Roman philosophers and medieval moralists and troubadours, here experiences the abandonment to God and his own powerlessness. The omnipresence of death in the place names inherited from the Middle Ages reminds us that crossing the pass was unquestionably a borderline experience for the living.

On the whole, the Christian was better equipped than the Roman for understanding passage as a total spiritual experience, which involved terror but channelled it and rose above it to become a form of anticipation of the trying passage to "eternal life". For everything that constitutes the passage, from the distant vision of the summits to arrival at the port, finds its corollary in the Scriptures. Medieval Christianity largely appropriated the pass as a physical space, giving it the spiritual significance intended by the presence of the extreme or ultimate features in the rock.

The time of wonder and the age of reason

"Without being able to explain it to myself, the mountains, and their marvellous elevation strike our minds and fill them with admiration". In these astonishingly simple terms Simler the humanist announces the advent of modernity.

Beyond the horror the mountain inspires, which can only be known by going through the pass, it becomes a place of rapture and questioning. The author seems to explain this very well: elevation, height, vertigo have always made it the place of the divine presence. One "sacrifices to the true God on the mountain", as did Abraham and Moses. At a time when men in Europe were still killing each other over the truth of the Christian religion, Simler reserves his most rational, and most personal, explanation for the "pagans": the Greek and Roman poets who gave us "their ideas about Nature in the form of myths" and "imagined a host of mountain gods" who are its phantasmatic incarnation. But in the beginning, he asserts in a wholly modern way, it was our "senses", stimulated to the utmost by the immoderation and verticality of the site, that generate "enchantment", in addition to another noteworthy verticality: that of time. Indeed, Simler surmises that geological time indicates the measure of our existence as much as the mass of the summits and the depth of the peaks indicates the measure of our bodies.

This intuition had already taken shape in a legend reported by an Italian traveller in the 1460s: it claims that the astonishingly well-preserved remains of a seafaring vessel, with its entire crew, as if petrified, its sails and anchors "broken", was found in a mine in the Bernese Oberland. The traveller is said to have heard this account from several men who had discovered this "wonder".

No doubt one ought to be wary of legends, particularly when told by an Italian traveller in the twilight of the Middle Ages. As in *The Book of Wonders* by Marco Polo, another of this traveller's most illustrious compatriots, we can appreciate the inventiveness and innate sense of wonder in this tale; but we can also perceive in it an intuition that will develop into a certainty as soon as the story is told. For the authors, who had learned to read Homer, Virgil and the Bible, the mountain was in fact the very image of eternity: the "rock" of which we are "sure". Mount Zion is the "dwelling place" of the immutable Being, and the "mountain" can never be moved, except in spirit and by "faith" – evoking the very image of the miracle. At a time when the sacredness of the mountain appears to diminish, it tends to become for mankind what it really is: the very image of time and its upheavals. We suspect, and soon we will know, that the Alpine folds were born of titanic telluric clashes on the first morning of a new world – our own – at the end of an unimaginable upheaval that consummated the disappearance of the primordial continent. Here, the measure of time is immeasurable: even if we were able to date the phenomenon with precision, what could these alignments of zeros possibly mean to us behind figures rendered abstract by their enormity?

In a way, this is what the legend of the Italian traveller is telling us: the verticality, the solidity and the immobility of this environment are not just appearances, but they are, however, deceptive. The Alps were born of a colossal movement, the verticality of which is its clearest expression. This movement is fixed in layers in the successive folds that passers-by had plenty of time to observe as they made their way over the passes, in their own time frame, determined by their walking pace. And Simler was an attentive observer of this. He had no doubt that "Nature" had one day "edified" these "gigantic masses" and he wonders for what purpose. There is no longer any question of divinities here but of the forces of the type of "Nature" demonstrated by the peaks and slopes. And the mountanous relief whose slopes the route tackles becomes a phenomenon, the work of an active natural force. The reasons for this escape him, but the questioning prevails. If his aim is not "to discover the causes and reasons for all the things that Nature keeps hidden" – and indeed, how could he – he confines himself to "describing, as a historian, and systematically, the phenomena themselves".

It is this attitude, shared by the most astute minds of the time, that gave rise to modern science. Beyond the "amazement" that the traveller will experience in the environment of an Alpine pass, there is a reality, a set of "phenomena". The excessive qualities of this environment does not mean, however, that it is invested with the supernatural: on the contrary, it is characteristic of a hitherto unrecognized nature that is to be explored and understood, here more than anywhere else, because the Alps are the folds and seams of the fabric that constitutes "the world". The spiritual value of the mountains grows: the Alps are on the way to becoming a fascinating object of study. For the scientific mind, the Alpine pass will no longer be merely a place of passage, but a privileged route of access to the most stimulating of open-air laboratories.

An open-air laboratory

Two centuries later, the Bernese geologist and cartographer Gottlieb Sigmund Gruner (1717–1778) published *Die Eisgebirge des Schweizerlandes* (Bern, 1760). Remarkably illustrated with maps and drawings by Samuel Grimm (1733–1794), the work lists and describes the main glaciers in the Alps of central and eastern Switzerland and attempts to explain their origins.

Traced from the Grimsel and Furka Passes, some of the views reflect both a concern for accuracy and a sense of wonder at the heaps of rock and stone in the landscape in which the scientist sees active forces frozen in their millennia-old thrusts.

We can imagine the state of mind in which Gruner climbed the northern slopes of the Grimsel, before discovering something that no longer exists in our time, or nearly so: "the Grimsel ice valley" of the Lauter-Aar glacier, where, walking cautiously near Brandlammhorn, Gruner heard the murmur of the nascent river under the "pure ice". Absorbed in his study of this environment, with spyglass or magnifying glass in hand, the scientist eagerly explored the first bends of the river, and the following ones more slowly, to the chagrin of his assistants. From a terrifying, hideous backwater, the Grimsel emerged as a gigantic field of study offering the human mind a mineral equation with several unknowns. In this spirit of discovery, there was not the slightest mention of any difficulties of passage, monstrous landscape, danger of avalanche or terrifying gusts of wind.

For Gruner, study of the Alps in Switzerland "can contribute perhaps more than any other country to perfecting the theory of the terrestrial globe". By this is meant the theory of the formation of landforms and of the continents, which at the time was the subject of lively debate opposing naturalists and geologists in Western Europe. This is where the story of our Italian traveller's ghost ship comes full circle: in Gruner's view, Switzerland, like the rest of Europe, "was once covered by the sea", proof being that "on all the mountains of this country, including on the highest among them, we find an almost infinite number of petrified shells". Gruner also refers to the biblical Deluge, suspecting the Alps to be like the scar "of a sudden jolt that must have affected the entire globe". This approach gives new meaning to the excessive nature that characterizes the Alpine space for the traveller. But this excess is fundamentally no more reassuring than the excess that led the *peregrinus* to honour the tutelary divinity of the pass at its summit.

Overcoming the burden of the world

Among the many authors published by Simler in the sixteenth century, Conrad Gessner (1516–1565) is probably the most famous, and for us one of the most interesting. The letter in which he praised the mountain contains one of the most explicit accounts of a phenomenon that was new at the time and that we would be tempted to call, even then, tourism.

Gessner contrasts "men with heavy minds", who stay at home, holed up "like dormice", not lifting their eyes from the ground, to those who, like himself, prefer to observe "with the eyes of body and soul, the spectacle of this earthly paradise". And indeed, the mountain offers the most beautiful of spectacles: "the spirit" is "struck" and "enraptured" by it, the soul is "moved" by it, because "one finds in the mountain all the elements and diversity of nature to admire to the highest degree".

Gessner was a new kind of pilgrim: he sought and found in the Alpine environment what he needed to cure him of the "disease" of apathy that he castigated in the inhabitants of the plain, and from which he likely also suffered when confined to the city. Literally and figuratively, the mountain is a victory over "the monstrous burden of the earth". Its very elevation symbolizes the liberation from the heaviness of the world, and which the spirit will sense when contemplating the "spectacle", that will "captivate beyond all measure".

Gessner was one of the first known mountaineers of our time: he climbed peaks, and his account of the ascent of Mount Pilatus remains famous still. He did not seek transcendence in the sense that medieval pilgrims did; he sought a physical "paradise" as the outcome of a

Carriages on Albula Pass road

quest to nourish the "spirit" and the "mind" by coming into contact with the immeasurable. The experience is therefore genuinely "spiritual" in that interiority is transformed by exteriority, bringing intense psychic pleasure. This experience has the power to overcome the heaviness of the world within us, to tear us away from our animal and vegetative condition, thus fulfilling for a time our highest aspirations. But this exteriority, so necessary to the expansion of the ego, no longer belongs to the Invisible: on the contrary, it is a "spectacle", a representation that seems to play out "Nature" for us, and of which we are attentive and deserving witnesses.

The aesthetic quest and surpassing oneself

The Englishman Joseph Addison (1672–1719) ushered in the eighteenth century with a famous description of Switzerland, in which he said that the mountains inspired in him "an agreeable kind of horror". Pleasure and horror, the pleasure of horror. This is a new way of naming and understanding excess. The confrontation with the mountain generates an oceanic feeling, a panic in the original sense of the word, which will be sought out. This feeling of "horror" is no longer threatening and crossing a mountain pass is still the easiest way to test this.

After Addison, many travellers expressed the complexity of what they had experienced in what appeared to be contradictory terms. At the end of the eighteenth century, on his way to the Lötschberg, Marc-Théodore Bourrit (1739–1819) endured an unforgettable thunderstorm followed by a reprieve that disclosed the montrous peaks above him. He described the "frightening and yet magnificent scenes" by emphasizing the disproportionate nature of the various elements that constituted the "spectacle": "extraordinary", "surpassing", "bizarre", "prodigious height", "extreme astonishment", "image of oblivion", etc. All this constituted, strictly speaking, "another world" in which the human subject was indeed merely tolerated – proof being that he returned alive – and stimulated, but with which there was no connection.

Reaching the summit of the Rigi in the mid-nineteenth century, Victor Hugo summed it all up in one sentence: "I lay flat on my back on the edge of the precipice and turned my head to look into the abyss". The self, and the abyss: a direct confrontation that enriches and broadens the imagination, judging by the literary output of the author, who was about to begin writing *Les Contemplations* (1856).

The scientific quest: a confrontation with reality

Horace Bénédict de Saussure (1740–1799), a renowned scholar and highly esteemed mountaineer who reached the summit of Mont-Blanc (4,807 m) in 1787, using the technical means we can well imagine, wrote several personal reflections in his *Voyage dans les Alpes* (1779).

From the Dôle, which he had reached after crossing either the Faucille Pass or the Marchairuz Pass, contemplating the panorama of the mountain range emerging from the sea of clouds before him he discovered a "strange" and "terrible" sight. Gazing out, Lake Geneva and the plain were made invisible by a thick veil of cloud, it "seemed to him that he was alone on a rock in the midst of a turbulent sea, at great distance from a continent bordered by a long reef of inaccessible rock", before the veil dissipates, revealing the presence of mankind and reminding him once more of which century he was in. De Saussure views the scene as a poet, but his poetic vision is fed with geological data that the European scientific community had been gathering for several decades. "A tidal wave of thoughts" overcame the scientist before the "strange" and "terrible" spectacle of the Alps! Far from limiting the researcher and philosopher in him, he adds to the excessive nature of form and proportion by reflecting on the time frame and successive phases of mountain relief formation.

In one famous passage in which he recounts his ascent of Crammont (2,736 m), the geologist is impressed by the vision of this "formation": the primordial ocean, of which Lake Geneva could seem like a remnant to him, the formation of gigantic salt deposits and then the successive apparition of the different mountains emerging from the waters and the earth's fire raising enormous heaps of molten rock, dragging with the water in its wake "enormous blocks" of rock lining the surface of our plains today, here and there. This vision is in keeping with the geological models of the time, but it is Dantesque, illustrating, as much as the sea of clouds, a mental horizon of desolation recognizing that man has no part in all this, neither temporally nor spacially. Visiting the mountains beyond the passes was so fruitful for the researcher because he was able in a single glance to dissipate the doubts that years of work had not been able to elucidate. Yet this opened up an abyss for him, comparable to the one that Victor Hugo had contemplated.

On more than one occasion, de Saussure felt "a kind of terror" mingled with "a kind of attraction that is hard to resist". "Rest" and "profound silence", a landscape of "enigmatic masses" silhouetted against the horizon of "twinkling stars": "It seemed to me that I had survived the universe alone."

What is man, who feels and lives, compared to the immeasurable expanse of space and time? By the force of his "imagination", nourished by decades of research, de Saussure had the astonishing ability to abstract the Alpine environment from any human component or from any "human" element linking the landscape to the reality of his own time and life. In other words, in the course of these dazzling experiences he brings the landscape within the realm of its own reality, in which man has no place. The confrontation with the double abyss of space and time reveals all the precariousness of self. And no mountain god comes to help adjust man's heart to the immoderation of the earth that carries him.

Grimsel Lake

The pass and the origins syndrome, from the Enlightenment to Romanticism

The "progress" that affected urban mores from the eighteenth century onwards was not always experienced as such by "enlightened" minds in search of purity. The urban environment was the seat of reflection, literary circles, libraries, financial entrepreneurship and political decisions, it was where "progress" was conceived and lived; yet it was also a place of pestilence – in a time of deplorable hygienic conditions – of fashion, entertainment and "moral licence". Considered an evolution by some, for others it represented a perversion of the natural order.

At the height of the Enlightenment movement in Western Europe, a twenty-one-year-old naturalist from Bern, Albrecht von Haller (1708–1777), wrote a long poem that was destined to be a huge success: *Die Alpen*. In flowery style, the well-informed naturalist evokes the flora of the Bernese Oberland, punctuating his work with learned notations, evoking one and the same plant in both poetic fashion in the text and its description in Latin in the notes, thereby reviving the ancient tradition of the scientific poem.

This dual perspective, at once poetic and scientific, resulted in the publication being welcomed as "a serious ethnological study". According to Peter von Matt, "herein was the explosive force of Haller's poem. What it showed everyone was the very real existence of a Golden Age in the Swiss mountains".

The land whose beauty he sang was "shepherds' country". His focus was on the Bernese Oberland and the Engelberg valley, but the way of life he evoked could be extended to the whole of this "pastoral land", from Gruyère to Appenzell. The northern slopes of the Alps, criss-crossed by pass roads, had indeed for centuries been devoted to pastoral life and the cheese-making industry. Haller was the first to bring this to light. He considered the people of the pass environment as a model to be emulated at a time when, throughout Europe, and in all dimensions, new foundational principles and models were being sought in an effort to improve the lot of mankind.

From his very first lines, Haller claims to have found this model: "Try, mortals, to correct your fate". This cannot be achieved by technical progress and the development of the arts alone: for such progress, were it to succeed, would cause "you to remain poor in wealth and miserable in opulence", he warned. Material progress generates luxury and moral impoverishment. The "shepherds' lifestyle" is thus proposed as a counter role-model to the civilized option, or such was the temptation to dream it when imagining the radiant future to which the development of science and technology could lead us. Haller advocated a focus on the present, because this happy shepherd people did in fact exist: he "redirected the temporal axis ... to an ancient era that still exists in the Alpine valleys". On the national scale, this projection of a moral and social ideal in the figure of the "shepherd" was to have considerable impact: Haller associated the mountains with "the Confederation as a whole". The area surrounding the passes, understood in the broadest sense, that is the villages that dot the valleys leading up to the passes and the pastures that line the ramps, became the ideal habitat in which people live freely, in harmony with Nature and their own nature. This is the habitat with which the Swiss can and must identify, even if they have never been up there before. But the author also gives a universal scope to his message. The "shepherd" is the model of "man" living in the "state of nature".

Haller's vision is a projection and a utopia. Peter von Matt revealed its purpose clearly: "he sought to influence readers in the towns with overtures of an Alpine paradise". This projective approach is characteristic of man's relationship with the Alpine region in general.

Rousseau's utopia on the road to the passes

Another Swiss from the Plateau, Jean-Jacques Rousseau (1712–1778), also made this idealized Alpine vision his own, in his own way, thirty years later in his masterpiece novel *Julie ou la Nouvelle Héloïse* (1761). The main action takes place at the crossroads leading to mountain passes.

Situated in Clarens, between Lake Geneva and the foothills of the Alps on the main road linking France and Italy, the very location itself eloquently speaks of the tensions it relates. The London-Paris-Rome axis is turned, on the one hand, towards modernity, the arts, urbanity and progress: at the time of writing, Paris and London were the twin centres of the Enlightenment and symbolized the future of civilization. In the other direction, the axis leads to Rome, and beyond, to the Mediterranean world, that is to Greece and further still, to Jerusalem. Italy, Greece and the Holy Land represent the origins of civilization in every sense of the word.

For a century more, they would nourish the spirit of the many artists who passed through Clarens to cross the Great St Bernard Pass.

This axis, which unites the two poles of European civilization, plays a major role in the novel. Saint-Preux, the novel's young hero and Julie's unhappy lover, finds refuge in Paris, from where he exchanges numerous letters with his lover in Clarens. Through this exchange, another axis emerges: one uniting the waters of Lake Geneva with the Alps. On one side is the Jaman Pass (1,512 m), which farmers crossed to sell their cheese products whereas the other side of the valley harbours the lakeside world of fishermen, where they live in harmony with the natural elements. This is the axis of intimacy and authenticity: the intimacy of the lake, where the two lovers can be alone, and the authenticity of the mountain pastures, where the couple share the simple life of mountain farmers for a time. This rustic society has characteristics that bring it closer to primitive humanity, as envisioned after Haller: these include moral purity, innocence, frankness, benevolence and simplicity, which the two lovers will enjoy on the road to the pass.

The world into which Saint-Preux emigrates by taking the route of "civilization" is just the opposite. His – involuntary – union with a prostitute encountered in a Parisian salon clashes with the quality of love – chaste, pure and fulfilling – that he knew with Julie.

Beyond the love story, *La Nouvelle Héloïse* can be read as an allegory of the fate of modern man in general and of the tensions that tug at *homo helveticus* in particular: obliged to live on the Plateau and nostalgic for the mountain pastures which are not even his original environment, he nonetheless ends up identifying with them as soon as the semi-urban life and forced openness to the changing world are experienced as a loss. The pass road, beyond which one rarely ventures, leads to that original incipit space in which one finds oneself, and ultimately symbolizes it fully.

In search of *homo alpinus*

It is often on the fringes of the major Alpine routes that Rousseau's successors thought they had found preserved specimens of humanity: *homo alpinus*, the breeder, the forester, the porter, the muleteer crossing the passes or the peasant living permanently on the mountain pastures and in the high valleys, the man of another time and from an area that was preserved because it was difficult to access. He embodied everything that urbanity had come to take away from the bourgeois and the man of letters: authenticity in social relations, probity, sobriety of needs, reduced to the essentials and communion with natural forces. Several travellers bear witness to this irenic vision at the height of the Age of Enlightenment.

Marc-Théodore Bourrit, cantor of St Peter's Cathedral in Geneva, and pioneer explorer of the Alps who accompanied de Saussure on his ascent of Mont Blanc, believed he recognized in *homo alpinus* the man in the state of nature imagined by Haller and Rousseau.

Bourrit claimed he discovered a perfect specimen of *homo alpinus* at the summit of Balme Pass (2,203 m), linking Chamonix to the Valais: a shepherd sitting on a rock, dressed in a furry jacket, quiet and shy, a perfect "half-wild" man looking after his livestock. Bourrit noticed a "neatly bound" book sticking out of the man's pocket: it was the *History of Denmark* by Paul-Henri Mallet (1730–1807). The good man confided to him that "reading is his most pleasant occupation when he is on the mountain tending his flocks". Decidedly, the man on the pass nurtured all the finest qualities.

German poet Johann Wolfgang von Goethe (1749–1832) raised another man to this stature: William Tell, in whom the Swiss recognized themselves from the very outset. For the great poet, Central Switzerland was not a remote place, but on the contrary, a major communications hub. He makes Tell a muleteer, a guide by trade, transporting merchandise and travellers along the Gotthard route, as well as the symbol of a crossroads nation under constant threat of foreign domination, whose inhabitants fight without respite for their independence. Busy with other projects, the great poet proposed this material to his friend Friedrich von Schiller (1759–1805). Though Schiller never set foot in Switzerland, his play assured William Tell an international reputation. First performed in 1804 in Weimar, the play was a great success. Schiller portrayed Tell as a man in the state of nature, whose character he drew from the descriptions in Haller's poem. As another man of mountain passes and alpine pastures, Schiller's Tell complements Goethe's depiction in terms of purity, integrity and freedom, crystallizing in the figure of Tell the ideals of both the eighteenth and nineteenth centuries.

At that time, the Alpine pass environment was partially seen as the ideal place in which to draw strength for

Grimsel Pass road

collective spiritual and moral renewal. In the Romantic era, it transformed into a place for personal renewal.

The pass and the quest for the world

In the eighteenth century, Europe's cultural elite indulged in the "Grand Tour": cultivated young people from England, France and Germany completed their years of learning with a trip that was intended to be a formative experience, taking the most adventurous – and the wealthiest of them – to the Near and Far East, Egypt, the Ottoman Empire, Palestine, Persia and India. Most passed through Italy, and often stopped there. For all, the Gotthard, Great St Bernard and Simplon Passes – as well as the Brenner Pass – represented passage from one world to another. They were a final challenge to be met, a necessary confrontation with the savagery of the natural elements before plunging into the delights of a domesticated and benevolent environment dotted with agreeable towns where the eye could be trained to appreciate the most accomplished works of art and marvel at the world's most beautiful landscapes.

In the eighteenth century, Italy was approached at a distance, through the paintings of Nicolas Poussin (1594–1665) and Claude Lorrain (1600–1682), where light, land and sea are filled with mythological figures sung by Virgil and Homer, or with biblical characters. Then came time for personal experience of light and colour, so clear and so profound, and which are in fact the real subject of these masterworks. Rome and Florence are both conservatories of European art and the places where the art that is admired there flourished: here and there, the same light on the sea, the same succession of curves formed by hills dotted with cypress trees recalling those in a master painting. And the same enchantment in the golden evening hue projected onto the long walls of the Quirinal and Aventine palaces graced by the gaze of a Buonarroti or Claude Lorrain. Italy once again embodied the Hesperides, the fabulous land of the Sunset where, according to Greek mythology, three nymphs guard the sacred tree of youth whose fruit is offered to those who know by what ruse to take it.

One ought, therefore, pass through Switzerland's Alpine passes in a state of indifference, in haste or apprehension, for they represents the exact antithesis of Italy, to which the passes open access. In contrast, they are artless places whose deformed and monstrous nature may inspire terror or devotion, but not pique the interest of the aesthete in search of harmony. The Schöllenen Gorge is, at best, the Hundred-Headed Dragon, posted there by a wrathful goddess to prevent access to the Garden of the Fable. Or they are merely places to be crossed. In the sixteenth century, Michel de Montaigne said not a word about his crossing of the Alps. He interrupts his narrative on the Plateau, resuming in the Po Valley, where people live in charming, policed cities. The real subject of our humanist's interest is to be with and understand people, "their habits and reasons".

Learning to see: Goethe finds himself at the summit of the Gotthard

The Gotthard, and Switzerland more broadly, held a singular significance for Goethe. In his quest for Italy, he attempted the dreaded massif three times without ever crossing it, stopping at the summit, at best gazing out at the expanse at his feet, towards the Hesperides, before turning back. The first time was in 1774, for a woman who had stayed behind in Germany. The second time was in 1779, at the end of a "journey through the Alps" culminating at the Gotthard. The third attempt, in 1797, aimed to save him from a country criss-crossed by Bonaparte's armies. Editing of the texts he brought back is complex, extending well beyond the facts that they relate since the diary of the first voyage was published only at the end of Goethe's life, in 1831, in his intellectual autobiography, *From my Life: Poetry and Truth*. The poet finally crossed into Italy via the Brenner Pass in 1786, but not a word of it was mentioned in his account, which is fully occupied by Italy alone.

It is said that a man can do only one thing well in his life. Goethe's great achievement was to learn to see. To see without projecting the image of his own interiority onto the object; to welcome it entirely and faithfully, allowing the image to imprint itself in such a way that the ego disappears to mesh with what is seen. Goethe's experience of the Gotthard was foundational for him.

The young poet had first travelled through Switzerland as a man of his time: exalted, frenetic, projecting his inner turmoil into nature. Like his hero Werther, he remained resolutely foreign to the world through which he passed; a world that was only of value insofar as it reflected his own self. *The Sorrows of Young Werther* was published in 1774, a classic read for *Sturm und Drang* youth. A man of genius, Goethe had radically expressed a way of being and seeing that would nourish European Romanticism and the pictorial art of the first half of the following century. "We expect dragons to emerge from the Schöllenen Gorge," he says. This was how William Turner (1775–1851) would soon paint it.

Returning to the mountain passes four years later in the company of the young Duke of Weimar, Goethe learned to observe. His account of the climb up the Furka is of major interest. First, he tells us about the use of the main passes at that time. They were crossed in the snow, at risk to one's life, guided by men whose job it was to lead the way on perilous terrain and who were used to courting death. When not ensuring the passage of travellers, they would bring goatskins in the middle of winter, to sell in Hospental. In Realp, on the other flank, one guide recounts how, one winter, he came to the aid of a family whose father had frozen to death and whose body he brought down to the valley. Hunger had chased the family from their home and they had set out thinking they would find the means to survive on the other side of the mountain.

There is something timeless about this story: for Goethe, the mountain pass is what it has always been, a place of uncertainty, death and desolation that must be escaped, first by vanquishing its hold on oneself:

> *I'm convinced that a man who, on this journey, allows his imagination to take control of him would, without any apparent danger, die of anguish and fear.*

Stopping at a chalet along the path at the foot of the first ramps, they are welcomed by a pious woman who reads to them – in full – the legend of Saint Alexius. The emotion is great and overwhelms Goethe. Here "fortune dominates" "prudence" and "courage". How can we *not* rely on Providence in such circumstances? We think of the pilgrims for whom the pass fed their thirst for God, and of all those who suffered passage as a mortal ordeal. The description of the landscape they pass through the next day is striking: it is "the loneliest place on earth, an immense mountain desert".

But Goethe is not looking for the picturesque and does not surrender to the horror of the experience. His description of the landscape is astonishingly precise. Feelings are considered dangerous to the purity of observation; they must be defended against and composure maintained. It is essential to see things exactly as they are:

> *My eye and mind could grasp the objects, and as I was pure, the impression was nowhere contraried. The objects produced the effect they were intended to produce.*

Free at last from the chain of affects that had been holding him back four years earlier, he "easily grasped each object", and "grew richer without becoming weighed down". This experience of rigour and purity of observation is the result of a "self-emptying" (kenosis) and a form of emotional asceticism that the poet consciously practised throughout his journey, from pass to pass.

Two special moments seem to have overjoyed him: "at the foot of the immense Gemmi", the author of *Song of the Spirits over the Waters* (1779) was immersed in an ecstatic experience in the original sense of the word, quite distinct from medieval piety and of a different nature from the dread evoked by Silius Italicus. Watching the clouds at dusk move towards him from the top of the pass, Goethe not only praises the "indescribable beauty" of this aerial "merry-go-round", he analyses and dissects the atmospheric phenomenon, seeking to understand its singularity and to measure the evolution of his own feelings until he feels "the secret, eternal force of nature running through all our fibre". There is no place for imagination here: you have to embrace brute perception, until you merge with what you see at the most intimate level of self. This involves stepping outside oneself, or *extasis*, the sense of being perfectly in tune with the surrounding environment, if for just a moment. And the word *nous* is *de rigueur* here: this experience of awareness is universal, accessible to everyone. Recalling it will afford "a pleasant sensation to the whole of one's existence". No excess, no intoxication, no fear in such instances, contrary to what our "imagination" conjures if left unbridled. Man is indeed "the measure of all things", as the ancients said. For Goethe, the experience at the pass is that of the true measure of man, born to become one with the world.

A few weeks prior, Goethe had contemplated the Mont Blanc at dusk. He reported seeing with an intensity somewhat similar to that noted by de Saussure, "perceived as though on a much higher plane, our thoughts struggled to attach its roots to the earth". But this intensity is not, as in the case of Saussure, the fruit of an imagination capable of reading the entire history of the world in stone and ice. It is a matter of brute perception. The difficulty lies in allowing it to flow through us without being affected by our associations, feelings or knowledge. And it must be understood. Wherever the author was confronted with the "extraordinary" he tried to express the back-and-forth dynamic between mind and spirit, until such time as he became one with the object perceived.

At the end of this second journey, on the summit of the Gotthard, Goethe tried to capture the majestic landscape of the southern slopes in pencil, but couldn't. The distance between visual experience and its translation into pictorial art could not be bridged. But this crossing of the Alps was decisive for him. A few years later, finally reaching Italy, he wrote:

My practice – of looking at and deciphering all objects such as they intrinsically are – my faithfulness – allowing my eye to become light – and my abandonment of all pretence secretly make me profoundly happy.

The eye had become a perfectly translucent interface with the fullness of Reality, as long as it be guided and directed by "seeing" and deciphering in one gratuitous act. It is not a matter of pretending to make an artistic representation of it, but of achieving complete transparency in the "mystery" of intimate perception. For Goethe, the fruit of this new relationship with the world was not a pictorial achievement, which he had definitively given up trying to create, but rather a profound serenity and a new understanding of perception. From this renewed spirit came, in maturity, his great masterpieces and the theory of colour.

His third visit to the top of the pass, in 1797, bore the mark of this secret, long-lasting happiness. A discreet note evokes the decisive moment of arrival at the "Port": "Little by little we were approaching the summit. Marshes, mica sand, snow, everything around us was sparkling. Lakes." Pared down like an etching, this brief passage hints at the magic of the pure moment in the effervescence of light. No adjectives, no assessment, no judgement. Pure presence in what is seen. Once again, the Weimar poet would not descend the southern slopes: Bonaparte's troops were chasing the Austrians across the Lombardy plains. But Goethe had found himself on the Gotthard.

Gemmi Pass overlooking Leukerbad

The pass and the quest for selfhood

Some thirty years after Goethe's final visit to the Gotthard, Astolphe de Custine (1790–1857) published *Aloys ou le religieux du mont Saint-Bernard*. It's a simple story: a young man reaches the top of the pass and surrenders to the storm raging in this "appalling" place, invested by "the evil of the century"; he is saved nearly against his will by a canon (and his dog). The religious man, who is the very image of serenity, confides in the young man. Like him, he was once a tormented being before finding God and inner peace at the summit of the pass, where he intends to live the rest of his life.

The subject was dictated by the times: the Romantic Age was keen on dramatizing the throes of passion, melancholy and the impossibility of being in the world. In the midst of the restoration of monarchical order it was also necessary, after Chateaubriand (1768–1848), to contribute to rehabilitating the Christian religion along with the clergy in its service. Custine set to work. The great Alpine pass would be for him what the "deserts" of "Louisiana" were for Chateaubriand: a very real place where the most essential aspirations of a generation crystallize. With Custine, the mountain pass is twofold in nature: a place of terror and death, it is also one of the highest spiritual elevation, where man fulfils his destiny.

Reading the letters he wrote shortly after the publication of his novel, we understand that Custine's attraction to the pass is real. One year later, he crossed the Gotthard via Altdorf, offering his reflections which are among the most explicit concerning the spiritual dimension of the pass for men of his generation.

Custine contrasts the Alpine valley with the mid-mountain region and its "sensitive beauty" capable of inspiring the "poet" and "artist", with the summit – and hence the pass, accessed by the road – as a high place of "metaphysical truth". Up there, the senses are "disappointed", because the rawness and brute savagery of the mountains at that altitude do not cater to the sense of beauty. The dissonance, which wrung the poet's heart as he contemplated the summits from the valley, diminished until it was completely erased. The effervescent colours and harmonious forms disappear, giving way to a kind of monochromatic "chaos" where, by dint of kenosis and elevation, the mind eventually detaches itself from the "landscape" as it climbs the ramps until reaching "an abstract truth". Man is confronted with "the soul of nature", with the profound "mystery" of the elements that speak to him a unknown language.

The sanctuary awaiting at the pass invites the author to make it the very place where the "Christian philosophy" is expressed most clearly, in the same way that the canons aiding travellers in the Valais pass area became, in his words, "the Mont Saint-Bernard philosophers to whom access should be denied to the 'uninitiated'". No more "art" at the top of the pass, because art is a way of appropriating an external object. And art thrives on the profusion and harmony of form. Here, physical form tends to disappear: "man no longer looks within himself".

Custine invokes a medieval vision of the pass, with intense – Christian – religiosity, but reformulates it in keeping with his time. He situates the "sublime", an aesthetic dimension whose nebulous definition was the subject of great controversy in its time, at the top of the Gotthard and Great St Bernard Passes.

The aim is to define the object of pictorial art in its highest expression. In this effort, Switzerland is at the heart of the debate considering that the great artists and art theorists pass through Switzerland on their way to Italy. Custine's notion of the "sublime" is somewhat beyond what is considered picturesque, strange or monstrous. It is beyond form and colour; beyond aesthetics. Paradoxically, for him the sublime begins here, at the top of the pass, where art ends. The pass being beyond the visible, like a mirror. Climbing up to the pass is a necessary prerequisite for descending into ourselves, to the point of investing our own spiritual core. This is a major stage in the poetic dimension of the pass. However close it may seem to be to Goethe's vision, Custine's approach is in fact, perhaps, the exact opposite: in Custine's view, the visible world is abolished, whereas in Goethe's experience, the world is revealed in its purest essence.

The Gotthard and disenchantment with the world: Chateaubriand

Never is one more intrinsically oneself than in the vicinity of the major Alpine passes. And particularly the Gotthard. This is what emerges from the curious account by François-René de Chateaubriand of his Alpine crossing.

Staying in Altdorf two years after Custine, the "enchanter", as he was already known, was assailed by the vision of his youth. Having retired from "business" two years previously, he was fully engaged in his life's work, *Memoirs from Beyond the Grave*.

Berninastrasse and Piz Bellavista

"Tête Noire" passage

In a disillusioned look at life and career, haunted by an acute awareness of the passing of time and of the vanity of all things, he experienced the reminiscences of a mature man.

At ten o'clock one evening, a terrible summer thunderstorm broke out in the valley. The old man was suddenly overcome by the "passions" of his youth: the roar of the Reuss river opened up to "the bard of Armorica". He saw himself at the youngest age, when he was running around the woods of his native Brittany some forty years earlier, gripped by the beauty and mystery of the world: a cantor, a "bard" or minstrel, a poet such as Homer or Ossian: ageless, singing the bittersweet joy of being at home in the world. That night in August 1832 suddenly brought back the "lost treasures" of his youth: "never had he spoken so passionately" as that night. Approaching the pass has the virtue of summoning in him the "sylph of the Combourg woods", a chimerical fantasy image that the child created and infused with even more life. Muse, inspiration and even imagined interlocutor of the child-poet, the "Sylphide" embodies all the essential aspirations. She is a remedy to the "wave of passions" and reappeared for the first time, here in Altdorf, at this key moment in life. He addresses her in vehement terms. Then there is a knock on the door: he thinks he is opening it to her, but the caller is his own guide, a local muleteer come to signal it was time for departure.

The account of the climb is extremely accurate. It is Turner's painting of the Gotthard that the writer unfolds before our very eyes, in a style all his own. But something had changed. As early as 1832, Chateaubriand regrets that the opening of the new road and the construction of the new bridge have "smoothed" the way. Modern times were already apparent: the meandering and irregular, "bolder and more natural" gradient of the older route was "singularly more adventurous" than the newer version, he was discovering with regret. The powerful enchantment of the Gotthard was gone. Vivid memories of ancient times surged: "the barbarian hordes" and "Roman legions", "knights" and "priests" who had crossed there before. Back then there were not, as there are now, good inns at the Devil's Bridge and Hospental, where one could enjoy a glass of fine white wine while reading a newspaper. There is greater comfort today, certainly, but the soul feels none the better for it. For if there are now "fewer thieves on the Gotthard, there are more rascals". The splendour of it all appears to him in all its cruelty: the contrast merely emphasizes the trivial nature of today's world.

Beyond Hospental, the politician and astute observer of his times and its customs clearly sees that the Gotthard is truly a strategic place, that nodal point whose various facets he evokes so eloquently. A watershed, a border, a provider of nourishment, the Gotthard is all of these: "as it did for the ancient world, the sterile snow transforms into fertile reservoirs for the modern world". The Latin lands to the south are irrigated by the Rhône river, and the merchant and industrial republics in northern Europe are irrigated by the Rhine. In this magnificent expanse the Gotthard massif is rightfully situated at the start of the forthcoming century which will introduce the mass production of commercial goods and foodstuffs. Fairies and "Sylphs" make way for a concrete, geographical perspective. In place of the old Gotthard, the one of the Devil, of "knights and priests", the modern myth of the Gotthard promises facilitated transit and passage. As for the spiritual vision of the pass, "I have struggled to reach the top in search of the exaltation described by mountain-loving writers, but in vain". Chateaubriand experiences no spiritual elevation and still less any moral purification. What we find in the passes is what we bring there within us: "it's the youth of life, it's the people who make sites beautiful". The pass is thus emptied of any intrinsic meaning:

I climb the rocks in vain, my spirit is none the higher; I take with me the cares of the earth and the burden of human turpitude ... God appears no greater at the top of the mountain than he does from the bottom of the valley.

And his Muse, his capacity for wonder and for the absolute which he promised just the day before to take with him across Schöllenen Gorge, has abandoned him, never to return.

Nostalgia has always existed, certainly. But in Chateaubriand it occurs at a decisive moment in history and at a unique time in his life. The sudden appearance of the muleteer in place of his muse seems to have broken his enchantment with the world once and for all. It also marks a break in time. The Industrial Revolution is under way: the term itself will appear for the first time five years later, in 1837. It was during Chateaubriand's final crossing of the massif that the author of *Memoirs* seems to have become brutally aware of this breaking point, in spite of himself. Chateaubriand is no longer himself; at that very moment of brutal awareness, he appears to be experiencing the end of romanticism and a disenchantment with the world.

Shadows, destiny and the future

In November 1878 Arthur Rimbaud (1854–1891), "the man with the wind-blown soles", crosses the Gotthard Pass on foot for the second time. On the way up from Göschenen, he notices the workers' barracks, built for those boring the tunnel through the mountain in a deafening din. Times are changing, but this inspires in him no particular reflection. He does note a change, however, in that the entire valley is "heavily worked and at work". There are workers everywhere, workers' barracks, workshops and canteens near the entrance to the "famous tunnel". Sounds of "sawing and the pickaxe are almost everywhere", a sign of the times. But the local innkeeper remains faithful to the legends of the land: he offers travellers "peculiar mineral specimens that the Devil himself supposedly comes to the hilltops to buy and then sell in town". Dealings were flourishing, and embellished in local legend.

Soon, he notes, "one is doing nothing but dominating precipices". The Devil's Bridge is indeed a place of "remarkable horror" yet "not as beautiful as the *Via Mala* at Splügen", of which he possesses a "view" in his sitting room. He says no more about this Mecca of the "picturesque".

The man is a connoisseur: for the past five years he has been criss-crossing Europe in all directions: France, Italy, Belgium, Germany, Austria, always on foot, on the road, "like a bohemian". But also sailing to the distant Orient on the great liners: Batavia, the East Indies, and all the ports along the Spice Route where the liners called. Though still young, he is already a seasoned traveller. He revisited his poetry before vowing never to write again. He renounced art, and the world. He burned his life, by the soles of his feet in a radical quest. His narrative is concise, agitated, factual. He tells of his journey as though to a sedentary audience, but he says no more than what is.

He continues on his way. He is on foot, in winter, and about to cross the pass in the snow, as others have done before him since the dawn of time. He is on his way to Alexandria. The "famous tunnel" is decidedly one of the most spectacular examples of the kind of radical development under way in Europe: do away with the mountain, conquer it using mechanization and engineering; disregard the terrain, the snow, the fatigue of men and bolt through the Alpine barrier by plunging straight into, or almost straight into a dizzying cloud of smoke and screeching whistles on the other side, without even having sensed there was an obstacle in the way.

The "serious climb" soon begins, past Hospental. While workers drill up above through the damp rock of the mountain, the snow and snowdrifts plunge the Gotthard plateau into a torporific state. We climb in groups, as always, to be able to assist one other and to face, in solidarity, the fear generated by the increasingly opaque whiteness of our surroundings which soon covers everything. We grope our way forward: the signposts set in the stone along the way remain visible. But which way to go? Inevitably, we will take a wrong turn. We sink into the white snow deeply, up to the waist. Further along, a two-metre-high wall of snow overhangs the road, and soon everything disappears in "an atrocious storm of sleet". Impossible to see anything. No shadow, no road, no sky, no precipice, "nothing but whiteness to think about, to touch, to see or not to see". The only landmarks in sight are the "telegraph poles" and "the shadow of our own selves". Half a shadow, in fact: "we haven't seen our knees for a long time", half-buried in the snow into which we sometimes sink deeply, "up to our arms". The only sounds to emerge from this cottony mass are those of travellers crying out words of encouragement to one another. We are doing our utmost to move forward, "panting", for the "torment can bury us without too much effort", in only half an hour. Suddenly we see a "figure" emerging from the white opacity, proposing "a bowl of salt water" for one franc fifty, before the bulk of the hospice takes shape at the last moment, like a "pale shadow" behind a trench.

This text is probably the most lyrical of those available to us from the final period of Arthur Rimbaud's life. He will say nothing, or almost nothing, of the large cities in East Africa and the Orient that he will soon discover. He will share place names, sketches of figures encountered, a few numbers (he became an arms dealer), and notes on "native" customs, scribbled in passing for the contractors employing him. But there is nothing that suggests anything of his own experience or what he is seeking by crossing the Gotthard.

The man has become a mere "shadow" in this white firmament. The shadow image represents the loss of self and the dissolution sought after leaving all behind to embark on the way, having entrusted the manuscript of *Illuminations* to a friend. That text also presents an image of the absolute. It is in this absolute whiteness, where what exists is no more than a "shadow", that the young man's "enthusiasm" emerges. As for so many

Grimsel Pass. Oberhasli Electric Station

In the Schöllenen Gorge

others, to Rimbaud the Gotthard is a place of passage, where no actual event takes place but where Fate seems to have clearly signalled the words condensing our aspirations and the profound meaning of the "vigilant soul". His is fading, along with contour and colour, in the great white "torment" of sleet. He will find nothing more essential nor purer in Africa.

Arthur Rimbaud is not the only writer to have found himself at last by crossing the Gotthard. "King" Arthur's passage there marks a turning point, however. What "absolute" is still to be found there? Indeed, nearly a century after Goethe's passage, the din of tunnel drilling, explosive detonation and screeching power saws all hail the onset of a new "modernity". The "picturesque" has lost its appeal, a fantasy there is no point pursuing. Yet the pass continues to enchant those who cross it at the right time.

The Gotthard and the seal of fate: Conrad

Joseph Conrad (1857–1924) crossed the pass as a young man, in 1873. He had already lost his mother, and his father – one of the great figures of the Polish resistance against Russian domination, who died of exhaustion in deportation. Entrusted to the care of his uncle, he left Poland for Western Europe accompanied by his tutor. The most important encounter of his life awaited him there.

Like Rimbaud five years later, he walked by the barracks housing the tunnel workers. And stopped. He dined and slept there, delighted not to run into that "creature called a tourist ... the kind of people who have no foothold in everyday reality". Without knowing it, he longs for the experience of "real life", wanting to observe and understand others in their singularity, their profound and noble nature. At lunch one day, accompanied by his tutor, he sits down in the middle of a group of engineers working on a tunnel breakthrough. "My first contact with British humanity", he notes. One man among them stands out. The "Romanesque and mysterious man" with a strong Scottish accent resembles the old sailor type that Conrad would later meet at sea or in European and other ports. The man strikes him deeply without Conrad understanding why. He and his tutor leave the meal and continue their journey over the Furka Pass, and the story could have ended there.

Conrad had shared with his uncle his wish to become a seaman. This was madness for the descendant of one of Poland's oldest aristocratic families, landowners and "gentlemen-farmers" for generations, for whom the sea was an unknown – the place of shipwreck. His uncle, who had in the meantime become his guardian, had instructed Conrad's tutor, a young student from Krakow, to divert the young man from his folly. To facilitate this, they were both sent to France for a change of decor and to give the tutor, adored by Conrad, all the latitude he needed to gently influence the young man of inflexible resolve. In vain.

Having passed Andermatt on the way up the Furka Pass, Conrad silently listens to the gentle rebuking of his tutor, who yet again lists the arguments against Conrad's ambition. Conrad nearly gives in. But at the top of the pass, they again meet the Scottish engineer whose enthusiasm and hardy countenance remind Conrad of his initial choice. When the Scot and his guide reach Conrad and his tutor, the engineer steadfastly and bravely looks at the young man as though to convey something utterly essential. Conrad draws from this the strength needed to confide in his tutor in a manner that deeply touches the latter. The young tutor then stands up and says to Conrad: "you are an incorrigible, hopeless Don Quixote". From the Furka they continue on to Marseille, where Conrad will discover the sea, and even more importantly, seamen.

This anecdote may appear insignificant. Not so for Joseph Conrad: he writes of the episode in great detail in his memoirs, emphasizing the fact that his entire life had been decided "at the top of the Alpine pass", facing the Rhône glacier. And that it was at the foot of the Gotthard that he first saw the key figure who would provoke decisive changes a little later, on the ramps of the Furka:

> *Was it in the mystical order of things that the envoy of my destiny was sent to tip the scales at a critical moment, with the peaks of the Bernese Oberland serving as solemn and silent witnesses?*

"You don't come across an Englishman like that more than once in life". He served as the model for the great characters in Conrad's later work: *Lord Jim*, of course, but also Marlow and Kurtz in *Heart of Darkness* or Charles Gould in *Nostromo*. A paradigmatic *homo britannicus* who projects his will and confronts it with vast spaces in the world, at the risk of being broken but not defeated. Józef Teodor Konrad Korzeniowski became a sailor, first out of Marseille, then out of England, from where he sailed all the seas around the globe. English, which he heard spoken for the first time at the foot of the Gotthard, would become his first language. At the end of his career as an officer in the British merchant fleet, he was to publish one of the most outstanding literary works of the twentieth century under the name Joseph Conrad.

Nomad rather than farmer: the pass as an Opening

Visitors to the pass today are no longer enthused with the spirit of discovery. They merely pass by. What appears to prevail today, at best, is the personal experience rather than the mysterious aura of the place itself. One either meets one's "shadow", like Rimbaud, or "the mystical order of things" weaves together the threads of a destiny in the making.

Hermann Hesse (1877–1962) was one of the last great writers to portray the Pass as a highly symbolic place of universal significance, while at the same time recognizing its leading role in the development of his personality.

When he crosses the Gotthard once again in the summer of 1939 Europe is ablaze and bleeding. Having settled in Montagnola near Lugano six years earlier, he crossed the border between the German- and Italian-speaking regions. Architecture, language, landscape – everything changes upon crossing the Alps. But he doesn't dwell on the differences: instead, he expresses his joy at living in Switzerland, a country that has within its borders one of the most remarkable geographical and cultural boundaries that can be crossed without having to change countries. He has the "the deepest contempt for political borders", that become "important and sacred", impassable in times of war, transforming territories into "prisons" and "torments" for "nomads" like himself.

Hermann Hesse was born and grew up in a Europe in which state borders were virtual. To visit the spas on the shores of Lake Como or Lake Maggiore, neither he nor Thomas Mann nor Sigmund Freud needed to present a passport when crossing Austria, Germany, Switzerland and Italy before the First World War. Nor did Stephan Zweig. As a point of passage from one world to another Hesse considered the Alpine pass to be the most potent symbol of the unhindered flow of culture from one country to another. Whoever crosses a pass in this spirit "points to the future".

One had to be a visionary to harbour such thoughts in 1939. That summer, the Gotthard was already becoming the core of Switzerland's defence system: an impregnable bastion, a padlock, a symbol of forced internal withdrawal. In autumn of that year, Max Frisch, living in Ticino, made the most anxious and alarming statements upon seeing the massif turned into a fortress, "Seen from the summits, you don't get the impression that the world, this sum of enigmas, is made for the likes of man. Only he who has faith can still rejoice when beliefs collapse".

Hesse had faith in the future. He considered crossing the Alps more than merely crossing a border. At the Alpine passes in Ticino the traveller discovers "a quality of humanity reminiscent of childhood, simpler, more fervent, more joyful". The radiant light over the southern slopes of the Alps recalls the "ancient way of cultivating the soil", the faith of yore tinged with paganism and "remembrance of our final goal". For this German-Swiss national of Baltic origin, crossing the Alps evoked something akin to a migration or pilgrimage to the sources of human culture. First of all, Hesse appears to be a new iteration of the torchbearer "mountain writers", in the words of Chateaubriand, who, since the Renaissance, have sought to convey the purity and simplicity of the Alpine environment, and that are sorely lacking in the industrial cities of northern Europe. And in a sense, this is indeed so. More importantly, he considered free passage and passage itself to be for the "nomad" as opposed to the "peasant farmer", who will not cross the pass, rooted as he is in his land and family. Hesse, on the other hand, "takes his heart with him". So, he can exclaim: "How beautiful to cross such borders!" For him, crossing the Gotthard remains "the road to deliverance": in the spring of 1925, he decided to leave Bern and settle in Ticino without his wife. In so doing, he ended nearly a half century of fruitless attempts to adopt the "peasant farmer" way of life rooted in family and a sedentary lifestyle. It was a life he had wished for but had never been able to live. The pass and the Gotthard were to him a passage full of the "promise" of accomplishment. Hesse presents us with one of the ultimate examples of a highly personal view of the Alpine pass, graced with moral and spiritual significance.

PHOTOFOLIO I

Richard de Tscharner

Vue sur le Grimsel avec Finsteraarhorn (4,274 m) – Furka Pass (Valais)

Roche polie par les Glaces – Grimsel Pass (Bern)

Teufelsbrücke – Schöllenen Gorge (Uri)

Fascinante Tremola – Gotthard Pass (Ticino)

La Tour de Hospental – Gotthard road (Uri)

Les Pavés de 1831 – Gotthard Pass (Ticino)

Courage… – Stelvio Pass, Kehre 15 (Italy)

Paradis pour motards – Stelvio Pass (Italy)

Les Gastlosen – Jaun Pass (Bern)

Vue sur le Mt. Vélan, le soir – Great St Bernard Pass (Valais)

En compagnie de Cairns – San Bernardino Pass (Grisons)

San Bernardino – San Bernadino Pass (Grisons)

Cima di Reit – Stelvio Pass, Bormio side (Italy)

Le Temps long de la Terre – Col de la Croix (Vaud)

Cascades en aval du Balmgletscher – Gasterntal (Bern)

Les Gorges de Gondo – Simplon Pass (Valais)

Airolo et la Leventina – Airolo (Ticino)

Couvent bénédictin de Saint-Jean-des-Soeurs – Müstair (Grisons)

Pizzo Uccello – San Bernadino (Grisons)

Piz Bernina mit Biancograt – Bernina Pass road (Grisons)

Finsteraarhorn – Nufenen Pass (Valais)

Saint-Bernard de Menthon – Great St Bernard Pass (Italy)

Débris – Nufenen Pass (Valais), Rossbode

Barrière artisanale – San Bernadino Pass (Grisons)

Vue en direction d'Altdorf, Mätteli au premier plan – Gotthard Pass (Uri)

Val d'Alvra – Albula Pass (Grisons)

Les Douanes et le Pain de Sucre – Great St Bernard Hospice (Valais)

Via Spluga – Splügen Pass (Italy)

A la sueur de leur front – Gotthard Pass (Ticino)

Pizzi Grandinagia et Pizzo Cavagnöö – Nufenen Pass (Ticino)

Les Traces d'un long hiver – Nufenen Pass (Valais)

Sportifs d'élite à l'entrainement – Furka Pass (Uri)

La Combe des Morts – Great St Bernard Pass (Valais)

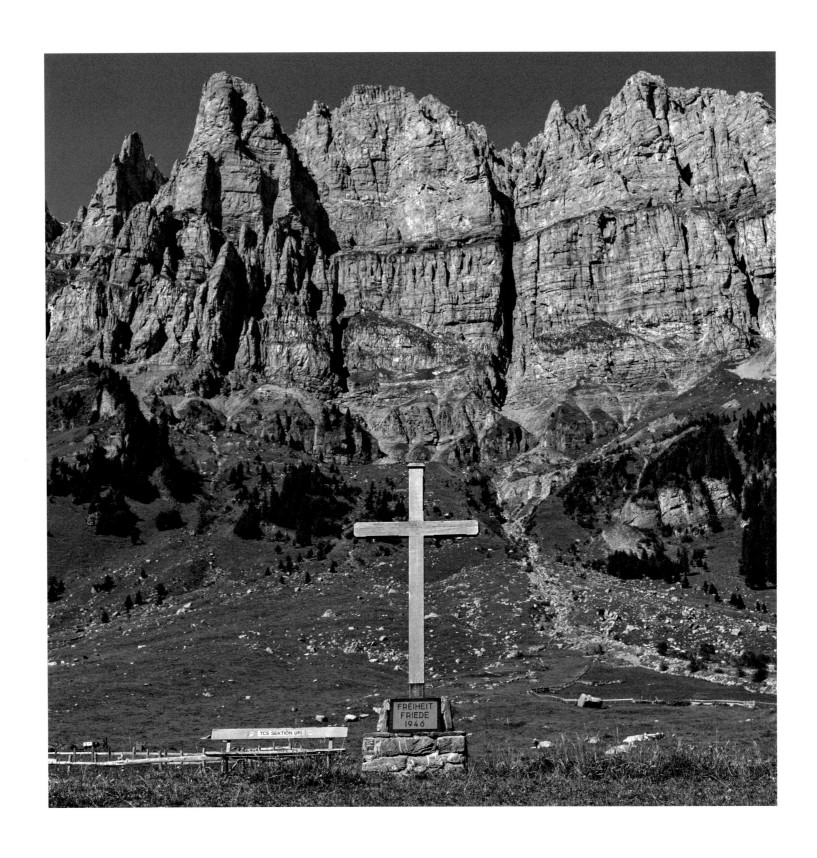

Freiheit Friede 1946 – Klausen Pass (Uri)

Barrage anti chars – Albula Pass (Grisons)

Souvenirs intemporels – Flüela Pass (Grisons)

Monumentale – Lukmanier Pass, Acquacalda (Ticino)

Acquacalda – Lukmanier Pass, Valle Santa Maria (Ticino)

Handegg, vue sur le Ritzlihorn – Grimsel Pass (Bern)

James Bond Street – Furka Pass Road (Uri)

Urserental – Hospental (Uri)

L'Hiver à la Bernina – Bernina Pass (Grisons)

Pierre vivante – Gotthard Pass (Ticino)

Brünberg – Grimsel Pass, Oberaar (Bern)

Ganter Bridge – Simplon Pass (Valais)

Le Barrage – Grimsel Pass (Bern)

Plis et Courbes au Stelvio – Stelvio Pass, Bormio side (Italy)

En attendant l'hiver – Gotthard Pass (Ticino)

Le Cercle des Glaciers disparus – Grimsel Pass, on the road to Oberaar (Bern)

Le Pain de Sucre et la Tour des Fous – Great St Bernard Pass (Italy)

Le Sommet par grand froid – Simplon Pass (Valais)

Granite lissé par les glaces – Rhône Glacier, Furka Pass (Valais)

Rhonegletscher – Rhône Glacier, Furka Pass (Valais)

Vue sur Gletsch et les Alpes valaisannes – Furka Pass road (Valais)

Val Muranza – Umbrail Pass (Grisons)

Ritzlihorn – Grimsel Pass (Bern)

Les Traces de l'Histoire – Schöllenen Gorge (Uri)

Il Viandante – Gotthard Pass (Ticino)

De col en col – Furka Pass (Uri)

Auf wolkigen Höhen – Oberalp Road (Uri)

L'Aigle du Simplon, symbole de vigilance – Simplon Pass (Valais)

ALPINE PASSES AND THEIR STRATEGIC IMPORTANCE IN THE PAST AND PRESENT

Daniel Lätsch

Forteresse militaire – Gotthard Pass (Ticino)

Introduction

Where the mountain separates, the pass connects. As the lowest point between two mountain slopes, it is the place where one can pass or cross from one slope to another. Hence the German word *Pass* was coined from the French *passer* via the Latin vulgar *passar*. Passes are essential travel and transport routes, mainly for trade purposes (map 1, p. 230) but also for military operations. The military importance of an Alpine pass depends primarily on two factors: whether there are strategic interests on the other side of the pass that warrant its use, and whether the pass can be crossed safely.

The most central and mythically charged Swiss pass, the St Gotthard Pass (hereinafter Gotthard Pass), wasn't crossable in ancient times from the north. This explains why Roman expansion into the Celtic areas beyond the Alps didn't take place over the Gotthard Pass but through the Rhône valley to the west and over the Septimer and Julier Passes to the east. It is therefore no coincidence that an early Roman cultural layer was discovered during archaeological excavations on the Julier Pass, whereas Roman traces are few and far between in the canton of Uri, where the "gold treasure of Erstfeld" (circa 300 BC) was unearthed, the most important find in Switzerland from the Celtic period.

The Gotthard Pass remained virtually impassable until the Middle Ages because the Schöllenen Gorge prevented access from the north. The few Roman coins found to date in the Urseren valley probably arrived via the Oberalp and Furka Passes rather than via the Gotthard Pass, as Valais, which was part of the Roman Empire, originally belonged to the province of Rhaetia.

It wasn't until the construction of a wooden footbridge around 1230 (replaced by a stone bridge in 1595 known as the Devil's Bridge) that the connection between the Urner Unterland and the Urseren valley was facilitated, and the Gotthard Pass gained in importance in the summer months. In winter, the Gotthard and Grisons passes could only be crossed by dint of considerable effort and additional risk.

Transalpine campaigns

Access to the Schöllenen Gorge eventually opened up new strategic possibilities for the people of Uri. Trade through the Gotthard and into the Milan region was boosted by the peace of 1331 between the Urseren valley and Leventina. This new connection triggered expansionist tendencies, which were facilitated by the Zurich pact of 1351: the extension of the aid circle up to Monte Piottino meant that the people of Uri could count on military support from the Canton of Zurich as far as Ambri-Piotta. In 1403, Uri concluded a protection treaty with Leventina, thus laying the grounds for the protectorate of Uri and Obwalden over northern Ticino and provoking a series of armed confrontations with the Dukes of Milan. The defeat of Uri in the Battle of Arbedo (1422) led to the loss of Leventina but didn't spell the end of Uri's expansion policy south of the Pre-Alps. At first, the people of Uri and their allies refrained from any aggression towards Bellinzona or attempt to conquer it. However, Uri succeeded in acquiring Leventina as a pledge in 1439–1441. Between 1447 and 1449, the people of Uri conducted several armed advances into Ticino and allied themselves with the lords of Locarno, and at times also with those of Lugano. It was only the defeat at Castiglione (1449) that stopped their progression towards Lombardy.

Not all Confederate cantons supported Uri's expansion beyond the Gotthard. Zurich's interests lay more with the access points to the Bündner passes. The Grisons aimed at territorial expansion towards Chiavenna, Valtellina and Bormio, whereas Bern and Valais advanced over the Simplon towards Domodossola. The Toggenburg inheritance dispute – also called the "Old Zurich War" – and the Burgundian Wars initially concentrated the strategic interest and military resources north of the Alps. In the course of the Burgundian Wars, the Confederates had encountered substantial Lombard mercenary contingents. The Duke of Milan's support of Charles the Bold (1433–1477) probably prompted the people of Uri to resume their expansion plans. By employing a ruse, a small contingent of Confederate troops, reinforced by about 400 Leventines, succeeded in putting the Duke of Milan's army of about 10,000 men to flight at Giornico (1478). The Confederate victory at Giornico forced the Milanese cathedral chapter to renounce its claims in Leventina. With the peace concluded in 1480, the new ducal dynasty of Milan, the Sforzas, recognized the rule of the people of Uri over Leventina.

The early cantons were not only interested in the Gotthard Pass and Leventina, but also in the Passo San Giacomo (2,313 m) further to the southeast, the Val Formazza (1,280 m) as well as the Val d'Ossola. Here, however, their interests overlapped with those of the inhabitants of Valais and Bern, who entered Northern Italy via the Simplon Pass and the Val d'Ossola.

The early cantons, along with the Valaisans and the Bernese, used the Alpine passes as transit routes, whether for economic purposes or to move armed contingents to the southern side of the Alps. The Gotthard axis, however, was not intended or even used as a defensive position. The battles in Ticino tended to be either raids or encounter battles. They took place almost exclusively in summer, because crossing the Gotthard Pass in winter with large contingents of troops was highly risky, if not impossible.

This situation remained unchanged at the time of the transalpine campaigns and Milanese Wars. The conflict began with the advance of the French King Charles VIII (1470–1498) into Italy. This ambitious young ruler was invited by Pope Innocent VIII (1432–1492) to take Naples. To this end, he rearmed his troops and reinforced his artillery with the most modern siege equipment of the time. Confederate mercenaries served in his army on the basis of the Perpetual Peace of 1452. However, the Confederacy became involved in the Milanese Wars through its own actions. In 1495, mercenary bands from Inner Switzerland occupied the Blenio valley and the Riviera. In 1500, they also took over the rule of Bellinzona (map 3, p. 234). The French King Louis XII (1462–1515) was thus confronted with a *fait accompli* and had to cede these territories to the early cantons in the Peace of Arona in 1503.

Matthäus Schiner (1465–1522), who ruled Valais at the time, openly advocated a coalition between Milan, the emperor and the pope, and tried to keep France away from Lombardy by all means. He therefore extended the armistice with Savoy for fifteen years in 1507, and in 1509 persuaded the Confederation to renounce the renewal of the alliance with France to conclude a pact with the Holy See the following year. In 1510, he convinced the Confederates to support Pope Julius II (1443–1513) in Northern Italy against France. A series of transalpine campaigns followed: the Pavia campaign in 1512, the battle of Novara in 1513, the defeat at Marignano in 1515, with consequences as dire as its human losses, the battle of Bicocca in 1522 and the second battle of Pavia in 1525. The Confederates fought as an independent war party until the defeat at Marignano, which led to them going repeatedly into battle against Confederate mercenaries. In the perpetual peace of 1516, the French King Francis I (1494–1547) granted the Confederates the land conquered south of the Alps, namely Locarno with the Maggia and Verzasca valleys, Lugano and the Mendrisiotto. However, the Val d'Ossola fell once more under the control of Milan.

The perpetual peace of 1516 was much more than just an open-ended peace treaty between the thirteen cantons of the Confederation and their allies (the Abbot and City of St Gallen, the Three Leagues, Valais and the City of Mulhouse), the French King Francis I and the Duke of Milan. The Confederates received hefty war reparations for the Dijon and Milan campaigns. At the same time, however, they had to give up their claim to the protectorate of Milan. This cemented the southern border of the Confederation for the next 300 years. The perpetual peace of 1516 was also an important step leading to the alliance with France in 1521 for the supply of mercenary contingents. Both treaties were an expression of the new balance of power in Europe and the Confederation's foreign policy orientation towards France. However, they were anything but the beginning of Swiss neutrality. It's true that they put an end to the Confederation's policy of expansion; at the same time, however, they made the Confederation largely dependent on the French kingdom. As a counterbalance, the Catholic cantons concluded similar treaties with Savoy in 1560, with the Holy See in 1565, and with Spain and Milan in 1588. These mercenary treaties not only brought new pensions and alliance money, but also improved economic conditions for the transalpine bailiwicks and the Gotthard transit.

Ticino had gradually become a common bailiwick since 1500. The bailiffs, who ruled over the bailiwicks, were elected to office by one of the sovereign cantons for two years according to a set rotation. In the event of war, they commanded the local troops provided by the valley communities. The Gotthard and Lukmanier Passes were now no longer just thoroughfares for large troop contingents, but also the connection between the thirteen cantons and the bailiwicks south of the Alps. In Ticino, whose defensive measures were mainly based on the existing castles and strongholds of Bellinzona, Locarno and Lugano, the need for military protection had also arisen. The Alpine passes remained lines of connection, at least in the summer months, and enabled the movement of troop contingents. However, they continued to play no role as barrier positions.

The Grisons passes during the Thirty Years' War

The Confederacy managed to remain largely spared by the Thirty Years' War due to a skilful strategy. Its readiness to defend itself, which the foreign powers regarded as determined, combined with a policy of non-interference and of supply of mercenaries, foodstuffs, horses and other goods essential to the war, saved it from being drawn into the conflict. The Grisons, on the other hand, whose von Planta and von Salis noble families maintained lucrative relations with Austria-Spain and France, respectively, were hit hard by the hostilities. Austria-Spain and France tried to gain control of the Grisons passes, the Valtellina being the shortest link between the Tyrol, which belonged to the Austrian Habsburgs, and Milan, which was controlled by the Spanish Habsburgs. Spain was also interested in these passes as crossing points between the Netherlands and Northern Italy, while the Protestants could only connect with Venice via the Splügen and Septimer Passes.

The Grisons Turmoil was triggered by the Sacro Macello massacre of 18–19 July 1620: Italian mercenaries killed some 500 Protestants and drove the Grisons ruling class out of the Valtellina. Spanish troops then occupied the area, while Austrian troops marched into the Val Müstair with the aim of securing the Umbrail Pass (map 5, p. 238). The Grisons counterattack failed a first time on 8 August 1620 at the battle of Morbegno, and again at the battle of Tirano about one month later.

In October 1621, Spanish-Habsburg troops invaded Prättigau via the Schlappiner Joch and Bergell via Chiavenna. At the same time, Austrian Colonel Alois Baldiron (†1632) advanced through the Val S-charl into the Lower Engadin and then via Davos to Chur. The Three Leagues were forced to sign the Milanese treaties, by which they not only had to renounce the Val Müstair, the Lower Engadine, Davos, Schanfigg and Maienfeld, but were also obliged to pay a fine and accept an imperial occupation (map 6, p. 240).

France, which saw itself threatened by the Habsburg successes in Spain, sent an army to Grisons in 1624 under the leadership of General François-Annibal d'Estrées (1573–1670), Marquis of Coeuvre. Together with the Confederate army, the French forced the occupying Austrian troops to withdraw. Owing to the Huguenot conflict, however, Armand-Jean du Plessis, Cardinal Richelieu (1585–1642), was compelled to reach an agreement with Spain with the Treaty of Monzon of 5 March 1626. After France had defeated the Huguenots militarily in 1628, it declared war on Spain. The Austrian troops then left the Rhine valley at St Gallen and headed for Grisons, looting everything in their path, occupying Chur and marching over the Grisons passes into Italy. But the war in Italy was unsuccessful for the Austrians and they had to conclude the peace of Cherasco with France on 6 April 1631, which obliged them to vacate the Grisons passes. France sought to permanently remove the Grisons passes from Austria's grasp and sent Duke Henry of Rohan (1579–1638), one of its most capable generals, to Grisons. Before the Austrian and Spanish troops could react, Henry of Rohan occupied the Valtellina. In the "mountain campaign" that followed, he succeeded in defeating the two enemy armies separately thanks to agile leadership and outstanding troop mobility (map 7, p. 242). Grisons immediately demanded the return of its former subject territories, but Cardinal Richelieu refused.

Subsequently, the Three Leagues forming the "Kettenbund" rose up against the French occupation. Jürg Jenatsch (1596–1639), who had converted to Catholicism for political reasons in 1635, occupied the "Rohanschanze" near Landquart with an army of 3,000 men and forced the French troops to surrender. In the capitulation document, Henry of Rohan had to promise the return of the Valtellina, which led him to be honourably discharged as an "honest man".

Jürg Jenatsch, then the most powerful man in Grisons, was ennobled by Philip IV of Spain (1605–1665). Following two years of difficult negotiations, the Three Leagues succeeded in concluding a peace treaty with Spain. The Milan capitulary of 1639 guaranteed the return of the Valtellina to Grisons, albeit with limited sovereign rights. Spain also promised military aid in the event of war and in return received the right to use the Grisons roads and passes as well as to recruit mercenaries. Jürg Jenatsch, who had made numerous enemies through his scheming politics, was murdered on 21 January 1639 and didn't live to see the signing of the treaty.

The Three Leagues had by then regained full foreign policy freedom as well as control over the Alpine passes. De facto, however, they were an Austro-Spanish protectorate.

The Alpine passes played a decisive role over the course of the almost twenty-year Grisons Turmoil. The Austrians and the Spaniards both, and Henry of Rohan in particular, used in their agile conduct of operations not only much-travelled passes such as the Flüela, the Julier, the Bernina and the Ofen, but also smaller mountain crossings like the Sertig (2,738 m), the Casana (2,692 m), the da Costainas (2,251 m) and the Chaschauna (2,694 m). In addition to being part of the movement and supply lines, the passes made it possible to circumvent the enemy and thus repeatedly created a decisive element of surprise.

Suvorov's Alpine crossing

The Gotthard Pass didn't become the scene of significant military operations until the war of the second coalition of 1799. After the French General André Masséna (1758–1817) attacked Grisons concentrically via the St Luzisteig, Oberalp, San Bernardino and Splügen Passes and forced the Austrian General Franz Xaver von Auffenberg (1744–1815) to abandon hostilities in the Chur area. After he had occupied the whole of Grisons, there were uprisings against the French occupying forces in that canton, as well as in Ticino and Central Switzerland. While the French troops put down the uprisings with much bloodshed, General Heinrich von Bellegarde (1756–1845) attacked the Valtellina and the Engadine coming from the Tyrol and pushed the French troops back into central and northern Grisons.

Simultaneous operations by Austro-Russian forces in Northern Italy forced the enemy to retreat north of the Gotthard.

The Allies then decided to deploy Austrian troops under Archduke Charles (1771–1847) on the Middle Rhine and to fight Masséna with Russian troops, while Friedrich von Hotze's (1739–1799) army corps were to continue to hold Grisons and the Glarus region until the arrival of General Suvorov's (1730–1800) army.

Suvorov began his advance on 8 September 1799 but chose as his approach the Gotthard Pass rather than the safe Splügen Pass. Just one day later, Masséna attacked Hotze's troops on the Linth and put them to flight. General von Hotze was killed in the process. Moreover, in the second battle of Zurich on 25 September, Masséna defeated Alexander Rimsky-Korsakov's (1753–1840) army, which retreated across the Rhine at Eglisau.

The preconditions for Suvorov's success were therefore no longer met. His troops encountered French resistance for the first time near Airolo. While France's troops were fighting delaying battles at the Gotthard Pass, a Russian detachment led by General Andrei Rosenberg (1739–1813) bypassed the enemy to the east and reached Andermatt via the Lukmanier and Oberalp Passes. Another circumvention over the Chrüzli Pass (2,346 m) led Russian contingents to Amsteg, in the rear of the enemy. After fierce fighting around the Devil's Bridge, Suvorov's troops advanced to Altdorf on 26 September. While the French troops held the Reuss bridge near Attinghausen, Suvorov decided to march over the Kinzig Pass (2,073 m) and the Muota valley to Schwyz. There, Suvorov learned that Rimsky-Korsakov had been defeated in Zurich. While a detachment of Suvorov's troops inflicted a severe defeat on the French troops under General Mortier (1768–1835) at the Muota Bridge, the bulk of the Russian troops escaped eastwards over the Pragel Pass (1,548 m) into the Glarus region. In the meantime, however, the French troops had occupied the northern exit from Glarus canton and Suvorov was forced to retreat over the snow-covered Panixer Pass (2,404 m) into the Anterior Rhine valley and to Chur. On 12 October 1799, Suvorov and his troops left Switzerland via the St Luzisteig and marched back to Russia via Munich. The Alpine campaign, accompanied by storms, snow and constant fighting, claimed heavy losses on both the Russian and French sides. The Swiss civilian population also suffered terribly from the hostilities. The foreign troops requisitioned food, claimed hay and grass for their pack animals and looted valuables.

In 1799, the Gotthard Pass – like the Kinzig, Pragel and Panix Passes – was only a transit route for the Allied troops and played no key military role. The decisions on how Suvorov was to cross the Alps were taken in Zurich or on the Linth plain. Swiss soldiers played no part in this. It is true that the French occupiers regularly recruited citizens of the Confederacy for their army. However, Swiss units weren't deployed during Suvorov's crossing of the Alps.

Napoleon's route over the Simplon Pass

For a long time, the strategic importance of the Simplon Pass was opposite to that of the Gotthard Pass. The Romans used the Simplon Pass as part of their network of major long-distance trade routes. It was used particularly intensively in the Middle Ages: until around 1320, the trade route connected the economic areas of Lombardy with the trade fairs in Champagne. However, tensions within Valais and the opening of the Schöllenen Gorge towards the end of the thirteenth century put an end to the transport of goods over the Simplon. The mule tracks were left to decay. During the Thirty Years' War, Kaspar Stockalper (1609–1691) discovered the importance of the Simplon Pass for the great powers, acquired a trading monopoly and in so doing created an enormous economic empire. Stockalper oversaw the construction of the so-called "Stockalperweg", or Stockalper path, as well as numerous warehouses. Nonetheless, the path remained a mule track and was never used for military purposes.

It was Napoleon (1769–1821) who first recognized the military potential of the Simplon route. In the aftermath of the Italian Wars of 1796–1797, he tried to obtain a right of way from the local authorities, but his ambitions went one step further: he wanted to have a road built over the Simplon as a link between France and the Cisalpine Republic. Construction didn't begin until 1801, however, so in May 1800 Napoleon led his reserve army of over 46,000 men not over the Simplon pass but across the Great St Bernard to Northern Italy and into the rear of the Austrian army. The construction of the Simplon road, inaugurated in 1805, subsequently benefitted the Allies rather than Napoleon. In June 1815, General Ferdinand von Bubna (1768–1825) led around 60,000 Austrian and Russian soldiers over the Simplon pass towards Savoy.

The military importance of the Simplon Pass remained relevant even after the Napoleonic period. On the one hand, the great powers decided at the Congress of Vienna to reintegrate Valais, which Napoleon had annexed to France in 1802, into the Confederacy. This was intended to remove the pass from the grasp of the great powers. On the other hand, the Confederacy had a first fortified wall built in the Gondo Gorge in 1815. But even after the opening of the Simplon tunnel in 1906, the army command attached only secondary importance to the Simplon Pass. Although the railway tunnel was equipped with mine chambers, the pass road was only minimally fortified, with a small infantry fort being built in the Gondo Gorge thanks to a residual allocation of barely 100,000 francs.

It was only with the emergence of the Fascist threat from Italy that the military importance of the Simplon Pass, which had been well developed in the meantime, as well as the smaller side passes, increased. In this context, Mountain Brigade 11, which was created in 1938, was supposed to defend and even block the Simplon Pass, but also numerous smaller passes such as the Monscera (2,102 m), the Furggu (1,872 m), the Alpje (2,092 m), the Albrun (2,408 m), the Chriegalp (2,536 m), the Grampiel (2,553 m) and even the Ritter (2,763 m).

Discovery of the Gotthard in the nineteenth century

With the adoption of the Defensional of Wil in 1647, the Federal Diet not only laid the foundations for the defence of Thurgau, but also for the long-term organization and arming of the federal army. For the first time, it was determined how many troops and guns each canton had to provide in the event of mobilization. Thanks to the peace of Westphalia, no mobilization was ever triggered based on the Defensional of Wil. However, after the situation worsened in 1664 due to the occupation of Franche-Comté by French troops, the Baden Diet decided to revise the Defensional. In 1674, the Diet officially declared the neutrality of the Confederacy for the first time. Although the Baden Defensional didn't remain in force for long, it was invoked by all the cantons – for the first and last time – at the Diet of May 1792 after the outbreak of the war of the first coalition. It also served during the Restoration as an important basis for the Federal Military Regulations of 1817. At the time, not only did the Diet define the competencies of the War Council and the contributions of the cantons to the federal army; it also created a General Staff and initiated a gradual centralization of troop training with the founding of the Central Military School in Thun and the training camps. In addition, it laid down standardized rules for the organization and equipment of the troops.

The first Colonel-Quartermaster of the Confederation, Colonel Hans Conrad Finsler (1765–1839), not only considered the deployment of the army, but also planned the consolidation of the fortification system. Finsler was convinced that a border cordon system, i.e., a chain of observation and guard posts, would be powerless in the event of a direct attack on Switzerland. He therefore postulated a "strategic central position", which was to encompass the Aare–Saane–Grimsel–Furka–Gotthard–Vorab–Walensee–Linth–Limmat regions. He described the defence of the Gotthard and the Urseren valley as "the first and strictest military duty of the Confederation". Nevertheless, the project was no longer pursued after Finsler's resignation as Colonel-Quartermaster and the first systematic national defence plan came to an end.

In 1832, Colonel Guillaume Henri Dufour (1787–1875) took over the post of Colonel-Quartermaster. His operational ideas only partially coincided with those of Finsler. He, too, envisaged a "vast entrenched camp", but this was to encompass only parts of the Central Plateau and the Pre-Alps. In addition, Dufour wanted to put up tough resistance in the border regions. He did, however, recognize the Urseren valley as a "bulwark of central Helvetia". Nonetheless, fortification work was carried out mainly in Aarberg, at Saint-Maurice and on the St Luzisteig.

It was only in response to the uprisings in the Austrian provinces of Lombardy and Veneto in 1848 that the Diet decided to call up a border guard corps and to grant an allocation for the expansion of the fortifications at Saint-Maurice, Bellinzona and on the St Luzisteig. Bellinzona in particular was strengthened because the Ticinese feared that reinforcement by troops from northern Switzerland would come too late in view of the poor north-south connections, especially since the Gotthard and San Bernardino passes were still barely crossable in winter despite the construction of roads.

In 1853, supporters of the Risorgimento attempted a coup in Milan, which was bloodily quashed by Field Marshal Radetzky (1766–1858). The Austrian monarchy, which suspected that the head of the revolution was in Ticino, closed the border to Switzerland and expelled 6,000 Ticinese. The Federal Council then requested an allocation of 200,000 francs for the reinforcement of the fortress structures near Bellinzona and on the St Luzisteig. It justified the allocation request not least by declaring that time had to be gained with the construction of the fortifications because, as long as there was neither a telegraph nor a railway line, it would not be possible to move troops to threatened points in the country in time. The parliament not only approved the request, but also granted a second allocation of 225,000 francs as well as additional advances. This made it possible to extend the defence line between Montagna and Sementina. The fortifications on the St Luzisteig and in Gondo on the Simplon road were also reinforced.

Between 1850 and 1880, national defence plans were drafted on several occasions. For example, the first adjutant of the Military Department, Lieutenant-Colonel Hans Wieland (1825–1864), proposed the expansion of several fortified locations in the Central Plateau, but also the development of Bellinzona into an entrenched base. Interestingly, however, it was a British officer, John L. A. Simmons (1821–1903), who recommended fortifying the Simplon and Gotthard passes.

The decisive change came with the opening of the Gotthard railway tunnel on 1 June 1882. The Gotthard axis was now crossable all year round. A few days before the opening, Italy had joined the Triple Alliance and the Italian General Staff developed plans to move troops through Switzerland to the Upper Rhine. The Great St Bernard and the Simplon Passes were first planned as marching routes, followed by the Gotthard Pass and later the Grisons passes. Federal Councillor Wilhelm Hertenstein (1825–1888) therefore called for the development of a territorial fortification concept based on a national defence plan. The National Defence Commission headed by Colonel Alphons Pfyffer von Altishofen (1834–1890) submitted its final report to the Federal Council in December 1882. In it, the commission proposed mainly massive field reinforcements and only a few permanent works. The Federal Council didn't take a decision until February 1885, but came out in favour of partial land fortifications and commissioned a study to strengthen Ticino and the Gotthard. Colonel Pfyffer's commission was in favour of expanding the fortifications at Bellinzona, securing the San Giacomo Pass with a construction at the level of Airolo and fortifying the Urseren valley in all directions.

For political and financial reasons, however, the Federal Council wanted to focus on fortifying the Gotthard tunnel's south exit and the Urnerloch, the southern access to the Schöllenen Gorge. Only small obstacles were to be built on the Gotthard, Furka and Oberalp passes. Despite resistance in parliament, technical difficulties and rapid technological progress, which called into question the planned works and led to considerable cost overruns, a large number of fortifications were built by the beginning of the First World War in the Airolo area and on the Gotthard Pass, as well as in Andermatt and on the Furka and Oberalp passes.

In 1892, the Federal Council designated the troops that were to defend the Gotthard fortifications. Two years later, by federal law, it also created a commanding staff under the leadership of a colonel, who was responsible for the defence of the Gotthard fortifications. With this, the Federal Council not only established a Fortification Command, but also troops that cultivated an outstanding esprit de corps and were endowed with a special sense of pride. The Gotthard Gunners, who wore a characteristic black beret in the early years, enjoyed an almost legendary reputation.

Even though the fortress structures suffered from considerable technical deficiencies, they were seen abroad as a clear expression of Switzerland's will to staunchly defend itself. At the same time, the country reinforced the moral value of "Fortress Gotthard" with the construction of the Gotthard fortifications. The Alpine Reduit concept was born.

The Gotthard Pass in the twentieth century: legend and reality

From the beginning of the twentieth century, technical developments and findings made the fortress structures appear obsolete. The first Chief of General Staff, Colonel Arnold Keller (1841–1934), already expressed doubts about the resistance of the various structures. The experience of the hostile parties in the First World War confirmed the fears that masonry fortifications would not withstand enemy artillery. For the time being, the Swiss army therefore only built field fortifications.

The traumatic experience of the First World War, the yearning for peace expressed in the motto "Never again war!", the hope for collective security through the League of Nations, the categorical rejection of national defence by the socialist party and the austerity mania of the bourgeois parties caused Swiss defence spending to drop to an all-time low. There was no thought of modernizing the army, let alone expanding the fortress structures. Only the rise of the National Socialists in Germany and the Fascists in Italy led to a gradual change in mindset. The procurement of modern weapons began too late, however, so that, at the beginning of the Second World War, the Swiss army had appalling capability gaps in almost all areas, but especially in armoured troops, anti-tank defence, artillery, signal troops, anti-aircraft defence and aviation. This said, the General Staff Service had recognized at an early stage that the combination of tank, infantry and airborne units made it possible to strike into the operational depths of enemy space and that there was therefore a danger of a "strategic assault". In particular, the General Staff Service feared a southern bypass of the Maginot Line by German or French attack units. It therefore pushed for the expansion of the border fortifications from 1934 onwards, but without considering the modernization of the existing fortifications at the Alpine passes.

After the outbreak of the Second World War, the Swiss army initially took up a standby or neutral position from which any enemy attack could have been countered. In October 1939, the commander-in-chief, General Henri Guisan (1874–1960), concentrated the infantry divisions in the army position which extended from Sargans across Lake Zurich and the Aargau Jura to the Gempen Plateau southeast of Basel. The southern front was to be defended by the 9th Division and Mountain Brigades 9, 10, 11 and 12. They were to fight until annihilation and at least hold the watershed, i.e., the Bernese Alps–Gotthard–Bündner valleys area.

In October 1939, General Guisan had a study prepared for the event of a simultaneous German and Italian attack. Additional resources weren't available for the defence of the southern front, however, unless the French army had rushed to help. The commander of Brigade 11 made it clear that the soldiers of Upper Valais would defend their valley on the national border and would never obey an order to retreat to the Bernese Alps. It is for this reason that, in his instructions of 4 December 1939, General Guisan demanded that the troops defend themselves for four weeks on the southern border, to delay the enemy, before withdrawing to the Sargans–Gotthard–Bernese Alps–Saint-Maurice line, where they had to defend themselves again. The rapid defeat of the French forces in May–June 1940 by the German Wehrmacht dramatically changed the Swiss army's situation. The country was now almost completely surrounded by Axis troops. There were simply not enough resources to defend the entire national territory from the borders. General Guisan therefore decided, in the event of an attack by the Axis powers, to concentrate Switzerland's defence in the upper Alps area with its important pass crossings, and the Gotthard Massif in particular, and to destroy all access routes to the mountains if necessary. The 9th Division, reinforced by Mountain Brigade 9, was given the task of holding the Gotthard, with heavy emphasis on the Bedretto–Airolo section, by securing the Val Bedretto, Airolo, the upper Leventina, the Val Piora and the Lukmanier Pass with advanced forces, and holding the Galenstock–Muttenhörner–Passo di Lucendro–Fort Airolo–Piz Borel–Scopi axis as the main line of defence.

In the Rütli Report of 25 July 1940, General Guisan explained his plan to the assembled senior staff officers and troop commanders. Far from being a simple statement of military orders, Guisan's speech was a call for unconditional resistance.

By August 1940, six divisions and three mountain brigades had moved into their operational areas in the National Reduit; from May 1941, the remaining three divisions joined them (map 9, p. 246). The border brigades were responsible for defending the frontier area and the light brigades for delaying the enemy on the Central Plateau. However, the bulk of the field army, consisting of some 240,000 men, defended the Pre-Alps and the approaches to the Alps, as well as the Alpine passes. Thus, the Alps and the Alpine passes gradually gained a firm place in military thinking.

Guisan's clear words in a time marked by uncertainty were of great symbolic value. The Rütli Report left its mark on the generation that lived through the Second World War and continued to have an impact beyond social barriers as an act of national self-assertion and cohesion after the war. This generation's will to resist was not only strengthened by Guisan's firm stance, but also by the politico-cultural movement of the Spiritual

Coupole de tourelle pour canon – Gotthard Pass (Ticino)

National Defence. The all-encompassing nature of the First World War had already led to the realization that national defence could only be successfully conducted with the inclusion of economic and cultural considerations. Because of the National Socialist threat, the Spiritual National Defence was strengthened even further and took on an anti-German character, especially in German-speaking Switzerland. From 1933 onwards, parliamentarians, intellectuals and media representatives called for cross-party measures to strengthen Switzerland's basic cultural values. Fritz Hauser (1884–1941), a socialist National Councillor from Basel, issued a postulate calling for the creation of *Pro Helvetia*, a cultural foundation whose purpose was to preserve the Swiss culture's spiritual independence. The Federal Council implemented the postulate in its message of 9 December 1938, stating that it was no coincidence that the first Swiss leagues were founded near the Gotthard Pass. The Gotthard both divides and unites three territories; it is an admirable fact that, around it, a great idea was born and became a political reality. The task of promoting the country's spiritual values was to be taken on by a foundation, *Pro Helvetia*, not by a state authority. The Confederation did, however, support civic education for children of compulsory school age with financial contributions and teaching materials. Barely a year later, General Guisan ordered the formation of the "Army and Home" section, responsible for keeping alive the troops' will to serve by means of lectures and entertainment, even during extended periods of military service. The most visible expression of the Spiritual National Defence, however, was the Swiss National Exhibition held in Zurich in 1939. The Gotthard was presented as the focal point and symbol of Switzerland. The efficiency of the country's industry was also demonstrated with the Ae 8/14 locomotive, which featured a futuristic streamlined design for the time and long remained the "most powerful locomotive in the world" with an output of 8,170 kWh. The Swiss Armed Forces Pavilion, the "Wehrbereitschaft" sculpture designed by artist Hans Brandenberger (1912–2003) and the military parades on the Zurich Allmend also impressively demonstrated the Swiss armed forces' readiness for defence.

However, the efforts of the Confederation, the army and private organizations couldn't conceal the fact that the army's withdrawal into the Reduit had arisen out of an emergency situation. Moreover, the army had very little time to move into the Reduit. The fighting positions as well as the command and logistics facilities had to be explored and expanded first. As a result, an intensive construction programme began quickly, in the course of which numerous bunkers, tank traps, command and fortification facilities as well as ammunition and equipment depots were built, especially along the transalpine routes and on the Alpine passes. With the Lona-Mondascia, Grandinagia, Foppa Grande, Stuei, Sasso da Pigna, San Carlo and Gütsch fortress structures, the Gotthard area moved to the centre of the defence deployment. It wasn't until the end of 1942, however, before a six-month supply to the population and the troops in the Reduit could be ensured and the most important fortifications completed.

Post-war period

At the end of the Second World War, an entirely new strategic situation arose. France and Italy were founding members of NATO, the defence alliance created in 1949 which Germany joined in 1955. Switzerland was thus surrounded by NATO members. Only the Soviet Union posed a threat at the time. An attack from the east through the Central Plateau was thus significantly more likely than a push over the Alpine passes. Still, the army stuck to the defence of the Alpine passes and deployed for this purpose the Mountain Army Corps with three mountain divisions, three fortress brigades, three Reduit brigades and three border brigades. During the "Army 95" reform, which took into account the disbanding of the Warsaw Pact, the army was to become a "modern, more mobile and above all even more versatile instrument of security policy". The static Reduit brigades and the border brigades were therefore disbanded. The defence mandate remained unchanged, and the required capability continued to be taught, but the defence mandate was coupled with the general preservation of living conditions and operational security commitments. In the Mountain Army Corps in particular, the mission of operational security commitments was implemented as protection for the transalpine routes. The latter were to be safeguarded in the interest of European goods transit, as well as of domestic Swiss passenger traffic and the transport of goods and energy. The surveillance of roads and viaducts, railway routes and energy carriers now took precedence.

The strategic situation in the European environment improved overall in the late twentieth century and the conventional military threat with a potential impact on Switzerland was perceived as "drastically reduced". The Federal Council consequently had the *Security Policy Report 2000* prepared, with the subheading Security through Cooperation. As before, but in a more flexible way than in the past, the aim was to ensure comprehensive cooperation between all Swiss civilian and military assets to safeguard security policy interests, take measures appropriate to the situation and be able to set defence priorities. Increased cooperation with international security organizations and friendly states should be sought, nevertheless. The leeway provided by the law of neutrality was to be used to the full. In plain language, this meant that the peace dividend approach should continue to be implemented, and political and diplomatic initiatives should be given greater weight than military defence efforts. The policy of dissuasion was to be replaced by a multi-pronged strategy of co-operation. The army was again subjected to a reform, and the number of soldiers reduced from 360,000 to 120,000. The so-called "Army XXI" was divided into brigades and battalions. The army corps and divisions were abolished, as were the fortified troops, and the fortress structures were decommissioned. The defence capability was only to serve to maintain expertise and as the basis for a possible "surge". In this context, the Alpine passes became at most axes of movement for a deployment near the borders.

The changing strategic importance of Alpine passes throughout history

To this day, the Swiss army's National Reduit dating from the Second World War and the post-war period enjoys almost legendary significance in the minds of the Swiss people. It is true that both the Reduit strategy and the national legend were called into question at the end of the twentieth century, mainly by left-wing politicians and young historians. But for the active-duty generation, the Reduit remained the epitome of the will to defend oneself. The number and size of the fortress structures in the Alpine region, combined with the long period of closely guarded secrecy, also increased the fascination of the Alpine fortifications for younger Swiss. An indication of this is the number of visitors to the fortress museums along the Alpine passes. However, both strategic location and defence technology have marginalized the Alpine passes. Today, the European states and their armed forces are part of NATO. Strategic interests lie in the urban agglomerations and along the main transversal routes through the Central Plateau. Modern weapons, including means of economic, cyber and information warfare, aim at a decisively larger, cross-border range as well as a considerably higher level of accuracy and impact. Defending from the Reduit – and thus at the Alpine passes – no longer appears to be expedient. A strategy that fails to protect the living and working centres of the Swiss people is no longer conceivable.

An aggressor or an alliance that would depend on the military use of the Alpine passes is also hardly conceivable, even when considering the most unlikely scenarios.

Thus, the Alpine passes remain part of Swiss geography, but also part of our history and our national legends. After having been difficult to cross until the Middle Ages, the passes were primarily used as trade and connecting routes for mercenaries in the late Middle Ages until the early modern era. During the Thirty Years' War and the Napoleonic Wars, the weakness of the Swiss military led to the passes being used mainly by foreign armies. It was only with the emergence of nation states in the nineteenth century and the construction of railway tunnels that the Alpine passes became more important for Swiss national defence. General Guisan's Alpine Reduit strategy, combined with the Spiritual National Defence, gave the Alpine region, and the Gotthard Pass in particular, a legendary significance that lasted long into the post-war period. Today, the mountains are crossed by efficient rail and road tunnels. Aside from some unsightly road and energy line constructions, our Alpine passes are once again integrated into nature and thus attract mainly tourists and hikers.

A VISION AND PROJECT OF THE CENTURY

Anton Affentranger

Real emotions shape the future – Sedrun (Grisons). In the access gallery of the Gotthard Base Tunnel.

From an impracticable Göschenen Gorge to the opening celebration

Wikipedia defines a mountain pass as "a navigable route through a mountain range or over a ridge … typically formed between two volcanic peaks or created by erosion from water or wind." A tunnel is defined as "an underground passageway, dug through surrounding soil, earth or rock, and enclosed except for the entrance and exit … for foot or vehicular road traffic, for rail traffic, or for a canal."

Both tunnel and pass connect, cross or literally pass over or under obstacles. A pass is basically defined by the terrain concerned. We use the natural configuration of the mountain terrain to determine where passage is possible. In the case of the tunnel, we burrow directly into the mountain with our hands and machines, building an underpass through the mountain.

At the Gotthard, the pass-and-tunnel duo has been part of a constant scramble for centuries. From the beginning, and for a very long time, the Schöllenen Gorge presented an insurmountable obstacle to access the Gotthard Pass from the north. It was only around 1230, with the construction of a footbridge over the gorge that "transit" over the Gotthard first became possible. Messengers, soldiers and goods thus found a quick way to the south or to the north. The Gotthard became a central European route. This pass naturally played a central role in the formation of the Swiss Confederation. It is hard to imagine that, without the Gotthard Pass, the initial regions could have mustered the strength to free themselves from the might of Europe.

The Gotthard Pass has shaped the north-south axis of Europe for centuries, with more than 10,000 people crossing it annually as early as the fifteenth century, and with the all too well-known summer "traffic jams" developing quickly, even in those days. Artists, too, were inspired by the Gotthard Pass crossing. Goethe crossed the Gotthard three times, describing and sketching his impressions in fascinating diaries. He inspired Schiller to use the "Wilhelm Tell Story", which he had heard on one of his Gotthard traverses, as literary material, giving rise to an important foundational element of Swiss identity.

Some 650 years after the construction of the first footbridge over the Schöllenen Gorge, the age of the railroad began. After heated debates at the "International Gotthard Conference" in 1869, political and business circles reached agreement on the construction of the first Gotthard railway tunnel. The project had to "overcome a sea of difficulties" before the vision and strength of Zurich entrepreneur Alfred Escher finally prevailed. Genevan engineer Louis Favre won the tender and built the approximately 15-km tunnel in just under ten years: an enormous technical, organizational and human achievement. Louis Favre and 199 others lost their lives at the construction site.

It is worth recollecting in a short aside that the celebrations of the tunnel opening were quite remarkable. Over 600 guests from all over Europe were invited to the inauguration ceremonies in Lucerne and Milan. A nine-course gastronomic meal was served on the occasion of the festive banquet given at the Schweizerhof Hotel in Lucerne on 22 May 1882 while the Lucerne Kurorchester played Weber, Strauss, Wagner and Verdi. On 28 May 1882, the newspaper *Landbote* wrote:

> Of the gentlemen who rejoiced over these days of completion of the Gotthard Railway in the complimentary party train and over champagne, few have any appreciable merit in the production of the work itself; but those who sacrificed their strength and sometimes their lives in the service of the enterprise were excluded.

Alfred Escher himself was among those who did not take part in the festivities.

In 1970, a century after the start of works on the first tunnel, construction of its Gotthard road counterpart began in earnest. It also took ten years to build, with nineteen workers killed during construction. Due to significant cost overruns, political authorities decided not to build the second tube and debate on the matter lasted for decades before the Swiss people finally agreed to its construction in 2016, on the strict condition that the tunnel be operated as a single lane only. Today, one naturally wonders how long this condition will last.

Towards the world's longest railway tunnel

Shortly after the Second World War, an initial concept for a Gotthard Base Tunnel was developed. At the beginning of the 1960s, the Federal Council commissioned the first projects and the KEA commission was established, the acronym standing for "Commission for a Rail Link through the Alps". The KEA studied several potential options, and the first exploratory drilling was initiated. In 1970, the KEA recommended a 45-km Gotthard Base Tunnel from Erstfeld to Biasca.

Intensive political discussions followed in the 1970s and well into the 1980s, with many variants put on the table. In 1988, five were proposed to the then Federal Councillor Adolf Ogi:

- Lötschberg – Simplon
- Gotthard
- Ypsilon (Gotthard variant + Bregenz – Chur – Erstfeld – Biasca)
- Splügen 1 (Bregenz – Sargans – Chur – Thusis – Chiavenna)
- Splügen 2 (Splügen 1 + Stuttgart/Singen – Zurich – Sargans variant)

In hindsight, some thirty-five years on, it is interesting to follow or at least try to understand the arguments for each variant. Many studies were conducted. Political lobbying in the respective regions was instrumental to the discussion and decision-making. From today's perspective, it is suprising that the decision-makers were not overly tempted by a variant wrought with compromises. Ultimately, the final decision opted for a rational and logical solution.

The NRLA – or New Rail Link through the Alps – has two north-south connections (Gotthard and Lötschberg) and correspondingly developed connecting lines. This both geographic and demographic logic was not disrupted by political considerations. The French-speaking part of Switzerland, which in principle was getting a somewhat raw deal with this route, nevertheless supported the project, thereby offering a good lesson in political foresight.

The population decides

At the heart of the storm
The years 1970 to 1990 could be considered as troubled for the NRLA. Several projects were examined and then rejected by the majority. The increasing clogging of the Alpine passes by lorry traffic was fuelling political tension. This period was also marked by increasingly tense political debate on Europe. The political and economic volatility led the Federal Council to declare in 1983 that "a new rail link through the Alps is not urgent". The project was thus put on ice until further notice.

Variants
A few years later, in 1989, the Federal Council decided to implement the so-called "network variant" (Gotthard and Lötschberg base tunnels). Federal Councillor Ogi sought to convince Parliament and Swiss citizens of the project's merit and gain their acceptance. In autumn 1991, Parliament approved the network variant. The result of a referendum held against this decision was extremely close and subsequently, on 27 September 1992, the Swiss population voted clearly in its favour (63.5%). The *vox populi* massively legitimized the project. Impressive as this was, funding for the project was not yet secured.

Voting by the people
At the time, Otto Stich, then Federal Councillor in charge of finance, expressed grave concerns about the project's financial viability. More years thus passed until Parliament approved the NRLA financing concept ("Financing of Public Transport Infrastructure Projects", or FinöV for short). The population had to vote on this, too, and the result was once again very clear. On 29 November 1998, 63.5% of the electorate approved the funding of the NRLA. The approval rate was identical to that initially voted six years earlier, with the Swiss population clearly recalling and remaining consistent in their stance. Only two months earlier, on 27 September 1998, the population had been asked about the LSVA (the "performance-related heavy vehicle charge"). The answer was likewise consistent; the citizens had demonstrated impressive wisdom.

Over a million visitors
People were keen to visit and experience the construction site and its advancement, and proudly report on this monumental project: over 1.1 million people visited the construction site. A modicum of pride could be expected in the circumstances of this rare opportunity to directly experience how tax money and levies are spent or invested.

Costs

It is not easy now to provide an unequivocal answer on the cost issue. While the original working hypotheses may have been valid then, the project developed significantly during the long planning phase and the equally long construction stage. During this period, there was a marked evolution in technology as well as in the framework conditions, naturally influencing both construction processes and safety requirements.

It is, however, worth casting a glance at the official figures from the Federal Office of Transport (FOT):

	In CHF billions
1998 referendum for the NRLA (Gotthard Base Tunnel and Lötschberg tunnel)	13.6
NRLA credit approved by Parliament	19.1
Current estimate at completion	17.7
Current estimate at completion at today's cost, including interest and VAT	22.8

One might naturally wonder whether the roughly CHF 20 billion (for the entire NRLA) was too much or too little. "The NRLA project is one of the best-controlled public projects in Switzerland", wrote Heinz Ehrbar and Peter Zbinden in *Tunnelling the Gotthard*, the ultimate reference work on the Gotthard Base Tunnel. Nonetheless, even sophisticated management processes combined with detailed controlling and reporting could not avoid the cost overruns. It should be noted, however, that the majority of the cost overruns were due to new requirements resulting from the development of needs and technology, as well as deliberate project changes. It was nonetheless possible to manage the project closely, objectively and in the interests of all parties involved. This was and remains one of the most decisive USPs ("Unique Selling Proposition") of this flagship project. The NRLA was built and is in operation today!

The initial economic effects of the NRLA have been remarkable:

- It has already led to a considerable increase in passenger traffic on the north-south axis (from around 6 million journeys per year in the "pre-NRLA" period to almost 12 million today).

- It brings about 20% more goods onto the railways. This corresponds to around 180,000 lorry journeys. The goal of shifting 650,000 lorries onto the railways is, however, still a long way off.

- The economic impact of the project is spread over two axes and regions (Lötschberg and Gotthard).

- Finally, the environment is a key beneficiary of the shift achieved by the NRLA.

Implementation

Pyramidal dimensions

It is difficult to do justice to the challenges of implementing a project of the size of the Gotthard Base Tunnel without resorting to comparisons. A total of about 28.2 million tons of material was excavated at the Gotthard, corresponding to five times the volume of the Cheops Pyramid in Giza.

Selected key figures

Length of the entire tunnel and gallery system	151.8 kilometres
Length of the Gotthard Base Tunnel	57.104 kilometres
Depth of Sedrun shaft	850 metres
Number of tunnel boring machines (TBM)	4
Length of TBM (Faido)	450 metres
Weight of TBM (Faido)	3,400 tons
Excavated material	28.2 million tons
Length of conveyor belts for transporting excavated material	Approx. 70 kilometres
Concrete consumption	4.0 million tons
Cement consumption	1.4 million tons

The above figures are impressive, each setting a record in its own right.

Clear processes and responsibilities

A project of this size could not be carried out successfully without the appropriate management. Alptransit Gotthard AG (ATG) – a wholly-owned subsidiary of SBB (Swiss Federal Railways) – assumed the role of project owner on behalf of the Swiss Confederation. From the beginning, ATG set itself a clear entrepreneurial goal and thus precisely defined the direction to be taken by all the partners involved.

We want the works on the Gotthard axis to be:

- of the agreed quality,
- completed as quickly as possible,
- and at optimal cost.

The ATG corporate goal

These quality-motivated goals formed the basis for defining a fully integrated management system. Support, core and management processes were defined and certified according to ISO standards. ATG was ISO 9001 certified as early as the end of 1997. The continuous improvement process was also regulated from the outset.

It is astonishing that clarity about the goals and processes was established very early on, before the project's actual construction. It was even more astonishing that not only were the goals defined but also – and this proved decisive – that everyone worked, learned and led according to these criteria for almost two decades. The resulting leading-by-example style management and corporate culture were deciding factors in the success of the project.

Challenges from the tunnel builder's perspective

The merger between Zschokke and Batigroup in 2005 gave the resulting Implenia Group responsibility for the construction of about two-thirds of the Gotthard Base Tunnel (Sedrun, Bodio and Faido construction lots). These billion-franc lots shaped the history as well as the future of the company for at least a decade.

Even though the lots were awarded to joint ventures consisting of experienced tunnel builders and the risks were thus better distributed, the risk profile of such large lots placed intensive technical, logistical and financial demands on the employees, management and board of directors of the leading partner, Implenia. The unanticipated geological risks that had to be overcome, especially in the southern part of the tunnel (Bodio, Faido), placed extraordinary demands on both the contractor and the project owner. In the course of the history of this construction site, countless challenges were added: whether these be the logistics in the Sedrun lot with the 850-metre-deep shaft and the construction of a multifunction station deep in the cavern; or the challenges with the 3,400-ton and approximately 450-metre-long tunnel boring machines and the overcoming of unexpected fault zones.

Breakthrough
On 15 October 2010, eleven years after construction began, an astonishing feat was achieved: the connection within the Gotthard Base Tunnel. The miners met up 27 kilometres from the north portal and 30 kilometres from the south portal. The precision of the breakthrough was also a world-class achievement, with a mere one-centimetre vertical deviation and eight centimetres horizontal.

People do make the difference
In the end, however, these challenges were overcome through the smooth interaction between the project owner and the tunnel builder. The rules were clear and above all based on mutual respect. The greatest esteem is nonetheless due to all the employees. If one were to single out only two individuals, they would be Arturo Henniger, who was responsible for the Bodio and Faido lots until 2005, the year of his untimely and sudden death; and how could we not mention Luzi Gruber – our "Mr. Gotthard" – who was responsible for the Bodio, Faido and Sedrun lots through to their successful completion.

St Barbara, patron saint of miners

The date of 4 December has been celebrated as the feast of St Barbara since the twelfth century. Although this date was removed from the Roman calendar at the Second Vatican Council, as the existence of this saint could not be confirmed, the feast day is still very popular today.

St Barbara has been the patron saint of miners for more than 300 years; in the Gotthard, the machines were shut down on 4 December.

What remains today?

This project catapulted our company into the "Champions League" of tunnel builders. It became a worldwide reference: a unique selling proposition that enabled the further development of the company.

Due recognition of the employees' contribution

In the peak years from 2005 to 2010, more than 2,000 men and women toiled on this iconic site. They included construction workers, miners, blasting specialists, machine operators, form-workers, commercial employees, engineers, environmental specialists, mechanics, geologists, foremen and many more. It is to them that we owe the construction of this tunnel.

Prayer to St Barbara (1780)

St Barbara, thou noble bride,
My body and soul to thee be entrusted,
Both in life and death,
Come to my aid in my final hour.

Come to my aid at my last end,
That I may receive the holy sacrament;
Drive the evil enemy far from me,
With your help remain forever with me!

I ask but one thing of God,
That I may die in His mercy.

When my soul is parted from my body,
Take it into thy hands,
Save it from the pains of hell,
And lead it into the kingdom of heaven.

Honneur aux souffrances des Hommes – Airolo (Ticino)

The result

At 57 kilometres, the Gotthard Base Tunnel is the world's longest railway tunnel. It is proof that it is still possible to turn great visions into reality. It should also be noted that the interplay between politics and business worked perfectly, which may be surprising at first. Ultimately, this project demonstrated that the "Swiss political model" is capable of extraordinary achievement.

In concrete terms, this means that Lugano can now be reached from Zurich in 1h 53m, or that it is conceivable to live in Italian-speaking Locarno and work in German-speaking Zug's Crypto-Valley.

And this is where this chapter comes full circle: the tunnel – the Gotthard tunnel – passes underneath obstacles and creates connections.

Key references
Tunnelling the Gotthard –
Erfolgsgeschichte Gotthard-Basistunnel, 2016 FGU
Specialist group for underground construction
(Fachgruppe für Untertagbau)
Heinz Ehrbar, Luzi R. Gruber, Alex Sala

Planning | Alptransit Portal (alptransit-portal.ch)
Swiss Confederation

Alfred Escher 1819–1882
Der Aufbruch zur modernen Schweiz
Verlag Neuer Zürcher Zeitung, 2006

PHOTOFOLIO II

Richard de Tscharner

Le glacier disparu – Furka road (Valais)

Gletsch avec l'ancien Hôtel Seiler Glacier du Rhône – Gletsch (Valais)

Ospizio km 5 – Gotthard Pass (Ticino)

Maison des Cantonniers et des Douanes – Stelvio Pass (Italy)

Premiers flocons – Oberalp Pass (Grisons)

Hotel – Furka Pass (Valais)

Der Origen-Turm auf dem Julier-Pass – Julier Pass (Grisons)

Mémorial au conflit 1914–1918 – Umbrail Pass (Grisons)

Panorama Diavolezza – Bernina Pass, Diavolezza (Grisons)

En descente – Nufenen Pass (Ticino)

Totensee im Nebel – Grimsel Pass (Valais)

Le col de la Furka avec un extrait d'une lettre de J.W. von Goethe de Suisse, 1779 – Furka Pass

Val Tremola – Gotthard Pass (Ticino)

Le Barrage Santa Maria – Lukmanier Pass (Grisons)

Monolithe – Grimsel Pass (Bern)

Lawienenkegel – Umbrail Pass (Grisons)

Gorges de l'Aar – Innertkirchen (Bern)

Le chantier du nouveau barrage de Spitallamm – Grimsel Pass (Bern)

Lumière matinale sur le Finsteraarhorn – Grimsel Pass (Bern)

Sept jours en Suisse… – Nufenen Pass (Valais)

AFTERWORD

AFTERWORD

Richard de Tscharner

As we crossed the legendary Great St Bernard Pass in the late afternoon on our way to Italy, I was once again awestruck by the magnificent high-altitude views and the atmospheric tones heralding the arrival of autumn. In this setting, I was suddenly enchanted by the thought of celebrating the beauty of the Alpine passes in a book of photographs, an idea I mentioned to my wife. This was in September 2016, at a time when I was no longer of an age to hike the mountains carrying heavy photo equipment. But many of the passes were now within reach by car; these rugged and authentic locations imbued with history were accessible. Looking out at the imposing Tour des Fous mountain before me, the idea took hold.

Delving deeper, I found that while there were many books about mountains and the history of mountaineering, there are surprisingly few publications about Alpine passes. One noteworthy exception is Julien Pevet's remarkable June 2017 memoir *Les cols des Alpes occidentales au siècle des Lumières (1740–1810)*. And yet when, in the eighteenth century, the Alps began to interest pioneers and scientists who first set out to conquer the summits, the mountains were still uncharted territory, whereas the Alpine passes were already decidedly marked by the travails of their past.

Several years ago, Frédéric Möri, a scholar, philosopher and professor of religion at the University of Fribourg, developed and coordinated the Orient-Occident and Alexandrie la Divine artistic projects with Professor Charles Mélà, then president of the Martin Bodmer Foundation in Geneva, for this library and museum recognized by UNESCO as a World Heritage institution, specializing in rare manuscripts and invaluable publications. He graciously agreed to place my photographs in a historical-cultural framework, and in September 2017 we found ourselves back at the Great St Bernard Pass, eager to get started on this book.

The immense Alpine range has been crossed at innumerable passes since the dawn of time, often in harrowing circumstances and conditions. In the interest of keeping to fathomable dimensions in this expanse, we chose to focus on the Alpine and transalpine passes on Swiss national territory as it was in 1815, when the cantons of Valais, Geneva and Neuchâtel joined the Swiss Confederation. We decided to concentrate on the historically important passes that lay along migratory, pilgrimage or trade routes, and notably certain strategic routes employed by armies in a Europe in the throes of change and theatre of many armed conflicts.

The largest mass emigration in the Middle Ages was that of the Walser people, who set out to colonize the Alpine regions located in what are today Switzerland, Italy, Liechtenstein, Austria and France. Several municipalities in the Alpine arc warmly welcomed migrants willing to engage in clearing and damming work. It is said that the Walser people, who settled in the upper part of the Reuss Valley – in Urseren between Realp and Andermatt – excelled in developing irrigation ducts and constructing footbridges on steep terrain. Around 1230, they used their know-how to build a wooden bridge clinging to the Kilchberg cliffside and spanning the Reuss river below. At that astonishing site, the famous Devil's Bridge was built of stone in 1587. This perilous passage across the Schöllenen Gorge, polished by ice more often than not, opened the way to the Gotthard Pass leading south of the Alps, which inevitably whetted the appetite of the Aargau-based Habsburgs who coveted the territory encompassing the Swiss Plateau and the Pre-Alps.

To defend their land, the rural communities of the Alpine pastures at the foot of the Gotthard range joined forces in 1291, inspired by a sense of pragmatism and the assurance that their triadic alliance would make them strong enough to stand up against the bellicose tendencies of the House of Habsburg. Symbolizing an innate desire for independence and freedom, this coalition became the precursor of the modern state of Switzerland, which, with the accession of Bern in 1353, developed into the Swiss Confederacy of eight cantons (map 2, p. 232).

It wasn't until 1386 at Sempach, near Lucerne, and 1388 at Näfels, in the canton of Glarus, that the Habsburgs retaliated against the Confederacy's increasingly strong aspirations for autonomy, but the Confederates remained united and ultimately emerged victorious, freeing themselves, for a time, from Austrian domination.

The development of the Confederacy was not without its setbacks. Although the common enemy, the House of Habsburg, had unified the Confederates, cantonal sovereignty gave rise to differences of opinion and competing alliances. In 1481, owing to the mediation of Niklaus von Flüe, later patron saint of Switzerland, a compromise was reached allowing the cities of Fribourg and Solothurn to join the Confederacy.

In 1474, the Perpetual Accord, a peace treaty, was signed at Constance between the House of Habsburg and the Confederacy, leading to a phase of détente after decades of conflict and tension. But the Confederacy's refusal to join the Swabian League in 1488 and to implement the reforms decided by the Diet of Worms in 1495 resulted in a bloody confrontation in 1499, won by the formidable Confederates, fighting to protect their hard-earned freedom against Swabian high nobility. The might and prowess of the Confederates were admired even by their enemies. Seven months of intensive warfare on the borders of the Confederacy had left Austria and Swabia in a state of ruin. This was the last armed conflict between the Confederacy and the Habsburgs, and the peace treaty signed the same year in Basel by Emperor Maximilian I represented de facto recognition of the independence of the Swiss cantons, marking a turning point in relations between the Holy Roman Empire and the Confederacy. Formal recognition, however, did not come until the signing of the Peace of Westphalia in 1648. One indirect effect of the Treaty of Basel was the admission of the cantons of Basel and Schaffhausen to Switzerland in 1501, followed by Appenzell in 1513. These events shaped the Confederacy of thirteen sovereign cantons, which remained unchanged until 1798 (map 4, p. 236).

Through his marriage to the daughter of the Duke of Milan, Emperor Maximilian I gained a foothold in Italy. The Confederacy was involved on account of the trade routes traversing the Alpine pass and the valleys south of the Gotthard, which were under Uri sovereignty. Moreover, territorial aspirations had led the Confederates to extend their zone of influence as far as Bellinzona (map 3, p. 234), and the alliance of the Three Leagues, allied to the Confederacy since 1498, occupied Valtellina, a strategic territory with access to the north over the Splügen, Septimer, Maloja, Julier and Umbrail Passes.

During the so-called Italian Wars, between 1494 and 1559, the Habsburgs fiercely opposed France's attempts to take control of Italy. Having acquired a reputation for invincibility, soldiers of the Confederacy were highly sollicited by the great powers of the time and, after the Burgundy wars, some cantons entered into mercenary contract arrangements, including one with the Holy See still in effect today. Against all expectations, however, in 1515 at Marignano, during the fifth confrontation of the Italian Wars, Swiss mercenaries defending the Duchy of Milan in the name of its young duke were crushed by a French army equipped with state-of-the-art artillery. Some 10,000 Swiss infantrymen died on the battlefield. Francis I of France became, during the first year of his reign and for some time thereafter, ruler of Lombardy. The expansion of the Confederacy towards the south ended with the signing of the "Perpetual Peace" agreement between France and the Confederacy of thirteen cantons in 1516 in Fribourg.

This first defeat reflected the disparate character of the thirteen sovereign cantons and their different cultural backgrounds, despite their seeming commonality. The decision to confront the troops of Francis I had not been unanimous, and although the mercenaries of Bern, Fribourg and Solothurn had returned to Switzerland, the other cantons had abided by the treaty that bound them to the Duke of Milan.

Four hundred years later, in 1915, in the midst of the First World War, Gonzague de Reynold, historian and great defender of the spirit of the Confederacy, warned about this harsh defeat in the *Journal de Genève* newspaper (13 September 1915): "The power of the Swiss was undermined by an evil to which we owe all the failures of our history: the disunity caused by egoism and competing regional identities, provoked by foreign influences. The campaign of 1515, where the fate of Switzerland as a European power was to be definitively decided, opened under the double sign of decadence and discord."

But let's return to our Alpine passes, where over the centuries a practice had developed of providing shelter to travellers often in distress, at least along the most highly travelled summits. Bernard de Menthon, born around 1020, canonized in 1681, was the first to build a hospice, at the treacherous Mont-Joux Pass and later at Colonne-Joux, to provide care and hospitality to all travellers, regardless of their station or religion. In gratitude, the local people changed the pagan names of the passes to Great St Bernard and Little St Bernard Passes. But this did not prevent some from perishing in the harsh and perilous conditions of Alpine passage; victims whose bodies had never been claimed lie in a nearby morgue, walled up after the Second World War. Many surrounding place names evoke the fatal perils of the area – Combe des Morts, Mont Mort, Totensee, Lago dei Morti and Cappella dei Morti – reminding those who venture there how suddenly the weather can deteriorate at these altitudes and become life-threatening.

In the years 1707–1708, as growing numbers of travellers crossed the Devil's Bridge to reach Andermatt, the first Alpine tunnel – the 64-metre-long Urnerloch – was built to replace the precarious footbridge running along the towering Kirchberg cliff. Around the same time in England, engineer Thomas Savery was developing a steam-powered device to pump water out of mines, announcing the arrival of the steam engine that would facilitate manufacturing processes in the earliest factories.

At the beginning of the nineteenth century, this invention transformed the mining regions of England, Wallonia and northern France from agrarian and artisan societies to industrial societies. The Industrial Revolution brought increased agricultural and industrial production, boosting trade between regions and countries. The development of railway networks was another consequence of the era, and in Switzerland, several rail projects across the Alps were being implemented. It was the tenacity of Alfred Escher, a Swiss politician, entrepreneur and visionary, that tipped the balance in favour of the Gotthard project. After ten years of colossal construction work, in 1882 a 15-kilometre-long tunnel was opened to traffic between Göschenen in the canton of Uri on the north side, and Airolo in the canton of Ticino on the south side. At Airolo train station, a monument honours the memory of the many victims of this herculean project, most of whom were Italian workers (see photograph on p. 180). The tunnel, financed by the German Empire and a unified Italy, ushered Switzerland into the new age of the Industrial Revolution. The federal state of Switzerland formed in 1848, succeeding the Confederacy of sovereign cantons. The circulation of goods was facilitated by abolishing inter-cantonal customs duties and introducing a national currency.

The mobility offered by technological developments and the expansion of rail and road networks gave rise to a new industry – tourism. Switzerland initially remained on the sidelines of the industrial advances, being almost entirely devoid of raw materials. It therefore welcomed tourists when they first appeared, mainly British initially but soon joined by visitors from other countries.

The merchant capitalism associated with these industrial transformations brought about a new social class, the bourgeoisie, with growing financial means to indulge many new desires. The relationship between man and nature gradually transformed, leading to a new appreciation for the mountains. The Alpine passes began to see many new types of visitors, ranging from wealthy families in search of pure mountain air, to artists, poets and scientists seeking inspiration and knowledge, to young aristocrats on journeys of initiation, to adventurers firmly set on conquering the highest peaks. Some travelled between the mountains on their way south while others made their way up to the heights and peaks.

While travelling for my photography project, which took me to parts of my country that I had rarely visited, I noticed how, in anticipation of a potential invasion, our passes had been equipped to slow down the advance of a dreaded aggressor. In June 1940, after the signing of the Franco-German and Franco-Italian armistices, when the high command of the Swiss army became aware of the strong likelihood of an impending attack on Swiss territory, the concept of the National Reduit first emerged. This defence system was based on a strategy of deterrence, providing for a series of fortresses and caves hewn into the rock of our Alps, capable of resisting attack. The Reduit grew into a resounding and rallying symbol of Swiss identity, of Switzerland's determination to resist its enemies, as it had always done. Today, some eighty years later, if you look closely at some of the details of our landscape, traces of this period can still be seen. One such emblematic site is the monumental granite sculpture at the top of the Simplon Pass, built by Mountain Brigade 11 towards the end of the Second World War, representing a sharp-eyed eagle standing nine metres tall, advocating vigilance at all times to safeguard our freedom (see photograph on p. 157).

The many tunnels built during the second half of the twentieth century gradually freed Alpine routes and broke with their nostalgic, stagecoach past to the delight of cyclists, motorcyclists and everyone who loves these magnificent regions, transforming the passes into adventurous or recreational destinations.

Photography of the Alpine passes also enabled me to reconnect with the beauty of the Bernese Alps and with Central Switzerland where it all began, as well as with the Grisons and the part of our country located in the southern Alps. I was thrilled to discover or in some cases revisit the legendary valleys leading to the passes, with their typical, picturesque villages. Not only did I travel through our country in different seasons, each featuring their array of colours, but I also journeyed through time, back to a period when Europe was being built. I realized just how much our mountain passes – which had been crossed over the ages by ecclesiastic and political dignitaries, armies and their commanders, merchants and traders, migrants, pilgrims and refugees – are an intrinsic feature of our history and cultural heritage. This book is intended especially for my Swiss compatriots and for all visitors to Switzerland who are interested in discovering the history of the Alpine region. I would like to ensure, despite today's comfortable, safe and fast means of travel through the mountains, that Swiss Alpine passes and their significance are given their due, and that their profound beauty continues to have a lasting impact.

Richard de Tscharner, Grimsel Pass (Bern)

PHOTO CAPTIONS

HISTORICAL PHOTOS

A note on the historical photographs, covering the first century of photographic practice in the Alps

From the earliest days of photography in the 1840s, photographers from all over Europe made their way to the Alps, lugging their cumbersome cameras and fragile glass plates, and sometimes even the copper plates required of the Daguerreotype process, deep into the remotest valleys and up to the highest peaks.

The panoply of these pioneering photographers included explorers, surveyors, mountaineers, scientists and shrewd businessmen who understood that dramatic Alpine imagery would have a ready market in less mountainous parts of the world. Although their work was often displayed in the newly-formed Alpine Clubs, in capitals such as London and Paris, it was exhibited less as prestigious artwork and more as vital information – providing a vivid window onto a sublime new world of rock, ice and snow, imagery perfectly suited to the needs of the Golden Age of Mountaineering.

Only in the early decades of the twentieth century would photographers begin to consciously consider their work as art. This period also saw the rise of popular illustrated magazines and the emergence of the professional photojournalist. But the turn of the century also marked the rapid rise of the amateur photographer — sometimes an inhabitant of the mountains or, more likely, a casual visitor. The early history of Alpine photography must acknowledge the considerable achievements of all these pioneering men and women.

William A. Ewing
Member of the Board, Carène Foundation
Curator, Carène Foundation Photography Collection

15 **The Great St Bernard Hospice and the Mont Vélan (Valais)**
1863
William England 1830–1896
Swiss National Museum
LM 805336 / GBE-39182

16 **Clearing of the Great St Bernard Pass road by the Hospice canons**
1935
Max Kettel 1902–1961
Nicolas Crispini Collection, Geneva

21 **The Old Hospice and the Barral House at Simplon Pass (Valais)**
1905
Arthur Wehrli 1876–1915
Swiss National Library,
Federal Archives of historic monuments:
Archives Photoglob-Wehrli
Transit at Simplon Pass significantly diminished after the Old Swiss Confederacy's defeat at Marignano in 1515. It was only during the Thirty Years' War that the route's potential was exploited by Kaspar von Stockalper, who built a hospice there to offer shelter to travellers. This "Altes Spittel" was in operation until the building of another hospice in 1831, commissioned by Napoleon Bonaparte. Below it is the Barral House, built in 1902 by the Savoyard priest Pierre-Marie Barral as a vacation home for missionaries. This unusual building, measuring 7 m. by 120 m. and initially serving as accommodation for seminarists, was purchased by the Swiss Armed Forces in 2007 for use as a barracks.

22 **Simplon Hospice (Valais) and Monte Leone, 3565 m.**
1905
Arthur Wehrli 1876–1915
Swiss National Library,
Federal Archives of historic monuments:
Archives Photoglob-Wehrli
Napoleon Bonaparte built the first carriage road over the Simplon Pass in the beginning of the nineteenth century, and also ordered the construction of the hospice. As a result of his downfall construction was delayed and completed only in 1831. Napoleon conferred the management of the hospice to the canons of the Great St Bernard Pass, who continue to operate it as a meeting place.

24 **The Devil's Bridge (Teufelsbrücke) and the Schöllenen**
ca. 1862
Francis Frith 1822–1898
ETH-Library Zürich, Image Archive
The Devil's Bridge was severely damaged in 1799 in a battle between French and Austro-Russian forces during the War of the Second Coalition. A new bridge was erected and in service only as of 1830. From then on, the original bridge visible in this photo was no longer used and finally collapsed on 2 August 1888.

25 **Schöllenen Gorge (Uri)**
1890–1895
Schroeder & Cie.
ETH-Library Zürich, Image Archive
(orig. Edit. Schroeder & Cie. Zürich)
Construction of the new Devil's Bridge in 1830 opened access to northern Italy via practicable traffic routes. From 1842, a daily carriage service was in operation. This photo illustrates the hairpin curves skirting the Schöllenen Gorge and gaining altitude to reach the Devil's Bridge.

27 **Simplon Pass road through the Gorge at Gondo (Valais)**
ca. 1855
G. Roman
Swiss National Museum
LM-100169.26 / GBE-13710

28 **Simplon road (Valais), Kaltwasser Gallery**
1895
anonymous
Schroeder & Co
ETH-Library Zürich, Image Archive
(orig. Edit. Schroeder & Cie. Zürich)

31 **Flüela Hospice, 2,388 m., and the Schwarzhorn, 3,150 m. (Grisons)**
ca. 1900
anonymous
ETH-Library Zürich, Image Archive
(orig. Edition Photoglob)
As in the case of the Julier, Bernina and Simplon Passes, Flüela Pass remains accessible year-round, outside of severe avalanche warnings. Constructed in 1868, the hospice building remains relatively unchanged today.

32 **At Furka Pass, postcoach and the Hotel Furka (Valais)**
ca. 1893–1918
anonymous
Swiss National Museum
LM-101478.35 / DIG-14154
Once the Furka Pass route became accessible to carriages in 1867, several hotels were built for tourists who came to admire the breathtaking panorama. The Furka Hotel was located at the summit of the pass until its demolition in 1982.

33 **Rhône Glacier, general view of the Grimsel and Furka roads (Valais)**
ca. 1890–1910
Wehrli Brothers
Swiss National Museum
LM-101401.78 / DIG-7986

36 **T.C.S. excursion by Gletsch, below the Furka Pass, 1913. Cars parked in front of the Hotel Belvédère.**
1913
Jules Decrauzat 1879–1960
© Keystone-SDA/Jules Decrauzat
The car park of the Hotel Belvédère is crowded; from the terrace of this luxurious mountain lodge, guests admire the Rhône Glacier, the local attraction, in 1913. Owing to the glacier's retreat, the hotel was closed in 2015 (see p. 190).

37 **Descending from Furka Pass (Valais)**
1921
Wilhelm Keller 1862-1947
Swiss National Museum
LM-91058.1 / GBE-133895
View of the Rhone Glacier and the Hotel Belvédère around 1921; see p. 185 for the same view a hundred years later.

41 **Military column on Julier Pass**
Winter 1914/15
Albert Steiner 1877–1965
Sammlung Fotostiftung Schweiz,
© 2022, Bruno Bischofberger, Meilen
Albert Steiner, a pioneer photographer in Switzerland, considered himself an artist and the technique of photography as a means of artistic creation.
Following his apprenticeship in photography in Thun, he worked for Fred Boissonnas in Geneva before opening his own studio there. Some years later he visited the Engadine and decided to establish himself there as a landscape photographer, reflecting his passion for the beauty and purity of nature.
In a career spanning forty-six years, his creation of works featuring the elegance of Swiss landscapes significantly contributed to the perception of Switzerland as an Alpine paradise.

52 **Tschingelhörner, seen from Segnes Pass (Grisons)**
1920
Jean Gaberell 1887–1949
Sammlung Fotostiftung Schweiz

55 **Passengers in an open-top postal bus**
1952
anonymous
Swiss National Museum LM-116483.4 /
ROH-2289 Studio PDL-Fotoagentur Presse
Diffusion Lausanne

56 **Man travelling alone on a mountain road**
1890–1936
Rudolf Zinggeler-Danioth 1864-1954
Swiss National Museum
LM-79763.75 / GBE-125330

61 **Survey of the Rhône Glacier**
1874
Emil August Friedrich
Nicola-Karlen 1840–1898
© Swiss Alpine Museum
Surveying conducted for the Glacier Commission in the summer of 1874 by Philipp Gosset, federal engineer.

62 **Carriages on Albula Pass road**
1901
Paul Montandon 1858–1948
© Swiss Alpine Museum

65 **Grimsel Lake (Bern)**
ca. 1885
Giorgio Sommer 1834–1914
ETH-Library Zürich, Image Archive
View on the Spittelnollen, where the famous Grimsel Hospice would eventually be inaugurated in 1932.
That same year, the Spitallamm (134 m.) and Seeuferegg dams were completed, resulting in a significant rise in the water level of the lake; the left side in this image, including the building, was entirely submerged.

68 Grimsel Pass road (Bern)
June 1936
anonymous (Kunstanstalt Brügger Meiringen)
© Swiss Alpine Museum
Excavation work on the avalanche cone on Grimsel Pass road in the so-called "Stäfeltichehr" below Seeuferegg.

72 Gemmi (Valais)
ca. 1900
Wehrli Brothers
Swiss National Museum
LM-146474.7 / GBE-45631
The Hotel Schwarenbach on the path over Gemmi Pass, with the Altels, 3,630 m., in the background.

73 Gemmi Pass overlooking Leukerbad (Valais)
ca. 1875–1900
Adolphe Braun & Cie
Swiss National Museum
LM-170958.19 / DIG-48419

75 Berninastrasse and Piz Bellavista (Grisons)
ca. 1905–1915
Wehrli Brothers
Nicolas Crispini Collection, Geneva
Postal stagecoach on the Bernina Pass road. In the background, Piz Bellavista, 3,922 m., and Morteratsch Glacier.

76 "Tête Noire" passage
ca. 1860–1870
Adolphe Braun 1812-1877
Sammlung Fotostiftung Schweiz
"Tête noire" passage on Forclaz Pass road between Châtelard and Trient (Valais).

79 Grimsel Pass (Bern)
Oberhasli Electric Station
1925–1935
anonymous
© Swiss Alpine Museum
The worksite of the Spitallamm dam (to the left) and Seeuferegg dam (to the right). The construction of these two dams, as well as the hospice, visible on the Spittelnollen, was completed in 1932. The hospice was all the rage at the time for having been the first establishment in Europe to be heated with electricity.

80 In the Schöllenen Gorge (Uri)
ca. 1909
anonymous
ETH-Library Zürich, Image Archive

PHOTOFOLIO I

87　View on the Grimsel with the Finsteraarhorn 4,274 m.
September 2018
Furka Pass (Valais)
View from the Furka Pass in the direction of Grimsel Pass. In the centre is the 4,272 m. Finsteraarhorn. To the left is the Oberaarhorn, 3,632 m., and to the right, the Agassizhorn, 3,947 m.

88　Rock polished by ice
September 2020
Grimsel Pass (Bern)
Climbing up the Hasli Valley to Grimsel Pass, near the Räterichsbodensee one can admire the view on this verdant rock polished by glaciers. In the background is the Alplistock, 2,894 m.

89　Devil's Bridge
October 2016
Schöllenen Gorge (Uri)
The Schöllenen Gorge and Devil's Bridge are historically emblematic of the entrance to the Urseren Valley and the Gotthard region. The Schöllenen Gorge was made accessible from around 1230 onwards, but it was not until 1595 that the first stone bridge was built. This infrastructure, however, suffered from heavy traffic and the forces of nature. Economic interests to the south and north of the Gotthard justified the investment needed to ensure the route would remain practicable. Construction of a new bridge was finally undertaken between 1818 and 1830, making the former mule track roadworthy for horse-drawn carriages and sleighs.

90　The fascinating Tremola
June 2017
Gotthard Pass (Ticino)

91　The Hospental Tower
September 2018
Gotthard road (Uri)

93　Paving stones of 1831
June 2019
Gotthard Pass (Ticino)
With the increase of traffic and construction of roads at the Simplon, Splügen and San Bernadino Passes, it was also necessary to plan a carriage-worthy road at the Gotthard Pass if it was to remain competitive. The difficult task of building a paved road was undertaken in 1820–1830, so that passengers, goods and mail could travel safely. Upon the opening of the railway tunnel in 1882 the road somewhat lost its importance, at least until the advent of the automobile in the twentieth century.

94　Courage…
June 2018
Stelvio Pass, Kehre 15 (Italy)
For a cyclist, the ascension of the Stelvio Pass is a feat comparable to a mountaineer climbing an 8,000 m. peak. Once the 2,757 m. pass appears after the Franzenshöhe, the cyclist must push his limits to persevere and reach the summit. The descent leads either towards Bormio in the Valtellina (Italy), or towards the Val Müstair in Grisons via the Umbrail Pass, at the top of which one enters Switzerland again.

95　Bikers' paradise
June 2018
Stelvio Pass (Italy)
Stelvio Pass, also known by its German name, Stilfser Joch, is the second-highest Alpine pass in Europe and as such, one of the most coveted by motorcyclists.

96　Gastlosen
August 2016
Jaun Pass (Bern)
Limestone range in the foothills of the Fribourg Alps.

97　Evening view of Mont Vélan
September 2016
Great St Bernard Pass (Valais)

98　In the company of cairns
September 2019
San Bernardino Pass (Grisons)
The layered flaky rock found all around the San Bernadino Pass is well suited for the construction of cairns. Such stacks of rock are traditionally used as markers along dangerous areas, indicating the way back along the trail.

99　San Bernardino
October 2017
San Bernardino Pass (Grisons)
The Laghetto Moesola is at the summit of San Bernadino Pass, which connects Bellinzona, in the canton of Ticino, to Thusis in the canton of Grisons.

100　Cima di Reit
June 2019
Stelvio Pass, Bormio side (Italy)
From the old road – no longer in use today – that connects Bormio to Umbrail Pass, or alternatively to Stelvio, one can admire the view on the Cima di Reit, 3,049 m., still marked by winter, accentuating its stratified rock structure.

102　The deep time of the Earth
August 2020
Col de la Croix (Vaud)
The geotope of the Chablais region showcases an Alpine landscape full of history: sediments on the flank of the Culan are clearly visible in the foreground. Time is measured here in millions of years. Even near the summit of the 3,209 m. Diablerets, in the background, the fossilized remains of marine fauna can be found.

103　Cascades below Balmgletscher
August 2017
Gasterntal (Bern)
A country road leads from Kandersteg towards Lötschen Pass and runs along the Gasterntal, a natural picturesque valley of the Bernese Oberland. It passes at the foot of the imposing wall of the Balmhorn, where one can admire the cascades running down from the glacier of the same name. As its name suggests, the pass leads to the Lötschental, located in the Valais.

104　Gondo Gorge
September 2019
Simplon Pass (Valais)
Along the Simplon Pass road the most impressive passage is undoubtedly that of the Gondo Gorge: a deep gash where the road, protected by a gallery, runs along the Diveria River upstream from the village of Gondo, the last town in Switzerland before the Italian border.

105　Airolo and the Leventina
June 2019
Airolo (Ticino)
View of Airolo, the southern portal of the first railway tunnel and the motorway tunnel that provide connections under the Gotthard Pass to Göschenen. In the foreground on the left is the expressway descending from the pass, and the Motto Bartola fortress. In the Leventina, the landing strip of Ambri airfield is visible.

106 **Benedictine Convent of Saint John**
August 2019
Müstair (Grisons)
This monastery dates back to the Carolingian era and was perhaps founded by Charlemagne. It offers a glimpse of the Middle Ages and the apex of the Christian era in the Renaissance. It is a composite of architectural styles from various eras that merge into a harmonious and aesthetic whole. Continuously inhabited throughout its more than 1,200 years of history, it was originally reserved for monks and became a Benedictine monastery in the twelfth century. It was listed as a UNESCO World Heritage Site in 1983.

107 **Pizzo Uccello**
September 2020
San Bernadino (Grisons)
The aesthetic pyramidal shape of Piz Uccello, 2,724 m., has made it the distinguishing feature of the village of San Bernardino. It is located to the north of the village and overlooks the pass of the same name.

109 **Piz Bernina and the Biancograt**
September 2020
Bernina Pass road (Grisons)
Piz Bernina, 4,048 m., with the steep white ridge of the Biancograt on the north side.

110 **Finsteraarhorn**
September 2019
Nufenen Pass (Valais)
A view from the Nufenen Pass on the Finsteraarhorn, 4,274 m.

111 **Statue of Saint Bernard of Menthon**
September 2016
Great St Bernard Pass (Italy)
Born around 1020 near Annecy, France, in what was then the Kingdom of Burgundy, Bernard of Menthon joined the Order of St Augustine, where he was subsequently ordained as a priest. While on mission in the Alpine parishes, he became aware of the great dangers of the mountain passes. He became the Archdeacon of Aosta and had hospices built at what was then known as the Mont-Joux and Colonne-Joux passes to offer shelter to travellers, regardless of their motivation or religion. In gratitude, the hospices were renamed after their benefactor.

112 **Debris**
September 2019
Nufenen Pass (Valais), Rossbode
Fragmented rocks and a tectonic mix at Nufenen Pass.

113 **Handmade Barrier**
October 2017
San Bernadino Pass (Grisons)

114 **View towards Altdorf, with Mätteli in the foreground**
September 2018
Gotthard Pass (Uri)
Travelling up the north side of the Gotthard between Hospental and the summit of the pass, along the boundary between the cantons of Uri and Ticino, one can get a glimpse of this beautiful valley carved by glaciers, with Mätteli in the centre.

115 **Val d'Alvra**
September 2019
Albula Pass (Grisons)
Looking towards Val d'Alvra (Romansh language for "Albula Valley"). Its beautiful plain is visible from the level of the pass, with the 3,199 m. Piz Blaisun on the left.

117 **The customs house and the Pain de Sucre**
August 2017
Great St Bernard Hospice (Valais)
In Roman times, this pass was the main communication axis directly to Gaul and the Rhine. During the reign of Emperor Claudius (10 BC–54 AD), a chariot road was built. Contrary to the other Alpine passes in use by the Romans at the time, this pass had no terrifying gorges to negotiate or abrupt rock barriers to pass over.

118 **Via Spluga**
September 2020
Splügen Pass (Italy)
The Via Spluga is a cultural trail that follows an old mule track tracing the long history of Spluga Pass, dating back to prehistoric times. After the Roman period, the history of the pass was defined by the links between the bishoprics of Chur and Como, and by the Lindau Messenger, a transport service between the cities of Lindau and Milan. The border with Italy is located at the pass itself. The road southwards was completed in 1822 by the Austrians, who ruled Milan at the time.

119 **By the sweat of their brow**
August 2020
Gotthard Pass (Ticino)
A gruelling climb on the paving stones of the Tremola.

120 **Pizzi Grandinagia and Pizzo Cavagnöö**
June 2019
Nufenen Pass (Ticino)

121 **Traces of a long winter**
June 2017
Nufenen Pass (Valais)
To the delight of drivers, motorcyclists and cyclists, the roads up to the passes were cleared at the beginning of June and progressively opened to traffic; traces of winter nonetheless remain visible.

122 **Elite athletes in training**
September 2019
Furka Pass (Uri)
Cross-country skiers must certainly appreciate the early snowfall, heralding the approaching winter. Members of the Swiss national team skate up the demanding climb to the Furkablick restaurant, seen on the horizon, in preparation for the first competitions of the winter season.

123 **Combe des Morts**
August 2017
Great St Bernard Pass (Valais)
The "Combe des Morts" is a small, enclosed valley dominated on both sides by steep slopes. It is located on the Swiss side and its crossing represents the final demanding climb before reaching the summit of the pass, where the Great St Bernard Hospice is nearly within reach. Due to the risk of avalanche and the tragedies that occurred there, the name Combe des Morts (Valley of the Dead) was adopted for this sector known previously as La Grande Combe.

124 **Freiheit Friede 1946**
September 2019
Klausen Pass (Uri)
The Urner Boden, a valley at 1,350 m. altitude, is the largest Alpine pasture in Switzerland. Inhabited all year round, it is located in the canton of Uri on the eastern side of Klausen Pass, on the way to Glarus.

125 **Anti-tank barricade**
September 2019
Albula Pass (Grisons)
In 1934, to delay or to stop the advance of the enemy forces, the Federal Council was instructed to give particular attention to the question of fortifications. As soon as construction techniques were updated, these works could be implemented and adapted to the newest techniques and weapons of war. As a result, the Alpine passes were equipped with permanent defences from 1937 onwards.

127 **Timeless memories**
August 2019
Flüela Pass (Grisons)
In the café of the Flüela Hospiz Hotel, the years 1939–1945 have not been forgotten; at the beginning of the war, Lieutenant General Henri Guisan was appointed General of the Swiss Armed Forces by the Federal Assembly. Following Switzerland's declaration of neutrality in the conflict, the army was mobilized to defend its borders for the duration of the Second World War.

128 **Monumental**
September 2019
Lukmanier Pass, Acquacalda (Ticino)
The work of the Alpine dairy farmers who ensure that high-altitude pastures and meadows are well maintained is highly appreciated. In summertime, their cows climb up to the heights of the passes to graze.

129 **Acquacalda**
September 2019
Lukmanier Pass, Valle Santa Maria (Ticino)
Lukmanier Pass, now mainly visited by tourists, connects the Anterior Rhine Valley in Grisons with the Santa Maria Valley in Ticino, and is passable all year round as it is situated at an altitude of only 1,915 m. The tiny village of Acquacalda is located 5 km from the pass at an altitude of 1,800 m., and provides access to a grandiose Alpine landscape, the starting point for numerous hikes to mountain lakes surrounded by rich Alpine flora and fauna, ancient Arolla pine trees and dolomitic rocks.

130 **Handegg, view of the Ritzlihorn**
September 2019
Grimsel Pass (Bern)
Above Handegg in the Haslital valley in the canton of Bern; a view on the Ritzlihorn from an Alpine pasture.

131 **James Bond Street**
September 2018
Furka Pass Road (Uri)
In 1964, the picturesque Furka Pass was one of the sites of the filming of the James Bond 007 movie *Goldfinger*. In memory of these unforgettable scenes a small section situated on the Andermatt side of the pass has a sign that reads "James Bond Str."; it is from this location that this photo was taken.

133 **Urserental**
September 2018
Hospental (Uri)
The Ursenen Valley in the canton of Uri is situated between the Furka Pass to the west, Oberalp Pass to the east and Gotthard Pass to the south, as well as the formidable Schöllenen Gorge to the north. The valley was isolated from the rest of the canton until the sixteenth century, when the stone bridge known as Teufelsbrücke (Devil's Bridge) was built.

134 **Winter at Bernina Pass**
January 2021
Bernina Pass (Grisons)

136 **Living stone**
June 2017
Gotthard Pass (Ticino)

137 **Brünberg**
September 2020
Grimsel Pass , Oberaar (Bern)
The Brünberg, 2,982 m., photographed from the Oberaar Dam. Grimselsee can be seen at the bottom.

138 **Ganter Bridge**
September 2019
Simplon Pass (Valais)
Development of the Simplon Pass road, to make it an operational and safe link to Ticino and Italy in winter, took place between 1960 and 1980 and required the construction of 5 km of galleries, 1.7 km of tunnels, and 24 bridges. The most spectacular structure on this route is the Ganter Bridge, which is 678 metres long. To the left is the old bridge erected during construction of the Simplon road in 1801–1805, as commanded by Napoleon Bonaparte.

139 **The Dam**
June 2018
Grimsel Pass (Bern)
The 113-metre-high Spitallamm Dam was constructed between 1925 and 1932.

140 **Folds and curves on the Stelvio**
August 2019
Stelvio Pass, Bormio side (Italy)
Impressive folds line the cliff face across from the old road leading to Bormio at Stelvio Pass.

141 **Waiting for winter**
September 2018
Gotthard Pass (Ticino)
Autumn ambiance in the Val Tremola.

142 **The Vanished Glaciers Society**
September 2019
Grimsel Pass, on the road to Oberaar (Bern)
On the road from Grimsel Pass to Oberaar: a view of the Lauteraarhorn, 4,042 m., and to the right, slightly hidden by a cloud, the Schreckhorn, 4,078 m. A similar photograph taken in 1874 during a survey of the Rhône Glacier by the Glacier Commission can be seen on p. 61.

144 **The Pain de Sucre and the Tour des Fous**
September 2016
Great St Bernard Pass (Italy)
View to the west from the Jupiter Plain, in Italian territory, of the Pain de Sucre, with the Tour des Fous in the foreground.

145 **The summit in cold weather**
January 2019
Simplon Pass (Valais)
The Tochuhorn seen from the Hospice at Simplon Pass. At 2,661 m., it is a prized destination for hikers in summer and skiers in winter.

146 **Granite polished by ice**
September 2019
Rhône Glacier, Furka Pass (Valais)
These granite rocks were crushed and filed down for thousands of years by the masses of ice that flowed slowly but relentlessly towards the valley. They then reappeared smoothly worn down after the recent retreat of the glacier.

147 Rhône Glacier
September 2019
Rhône Glacier, Furka Pass (Valais)
Since the middle of the nineteenth century the accelerating retreat of glaciers has become increasingly noticeable. The phenomenon has become of such concern as to introduce the technique of partially covering the glaciers with UV-resistant blankets aiming to slow the process and their ultimate disappearance.

149 View of Gletsch and the Valais Alps
September 2018
Furka Pass road (Valais)
From the Hotel Belvédère, on the Valais side of the Furka Pass, is a view of Gletsch with the Furka road on the left and Grimsel Pass road on the right. At the summit, the Totensee is just visible. In the background at left, the Alps of the Valais can be seen through the haze.

150 Val Muranza
August 2019
Umbrail Pass (Grisons)
Cloud formation at Umbrail Pass.

151 Ritzlihorn
September 2019
Grimsel Pass (Bern)
Morning view of the Ritzlihorn, 3,277 m., with the Räterichsbodensee in the foreground, below the Grimsel Hospiz Hotel.

152 Traces of history
August 2020
Schöllenen Gorge (Uri)
In 1595, a precarious structure dating from the 1230s was replaced by a stone bridge known as Devil's Bridge. It was severely damaged during the War of the Second Coalition in 1799, when Napoleon's troops clashed with those of Russian General Suvorov. The remains of its foundations are still visible today, however. A second bridge built in 1830 was used for traffic including motor vehicles until 1958, when a third bridge was opened exclusively for vehicular traffic.

153 Il Viandante
October 2016
Gotthard Pass (Ticino)
Not far from the Gotthard Hospice is this impressive sculpture by Pedro Pedrazzini, a Swiss artist born in 1953 who resides in Minusio, Ticino. Il Viandante is a wanderer with a serene Christ-like aura, his gaze fixed far into the horizon.

154 From pass to pass
September 2019
Furka Pass (Uri)
A view from the first curves of the Furka Pass into Urseren Valley, with Realp in the foreground, Andermatt at the other end of the valley and the climb up to Oberalp Pass.

155 On cloudy heights
June 2017
Oberalp Road (Uri)
At dusk on the way from Andermatt to Oberalp Pass: a dreamy moment that evokes Richard Strauss's *An Alpine Symphony*.

157 The Simplon Eagle: symbol of vigilance
September 2020
Simplon Pass (Valais)
The Simplon Eagle was erected in 1944 by Swiss Mountain Brigade 11, in the framework of the defensive strategy known as the "National Reduit" during the Second World War. The eagle's gaze facing south symbolizes the duty of vigilance and loyalty to the homeland. At its base is the following inscription: *"In the freedom of the mountains, a massive imprint in hard granite: a reminder of accomplished duty, a permanent warning to be willing and attentive to our freedom"*.

160 Military fortress
October 2016
Gotthard Pass (Ticino)
With the development of the road network in the mid-nineteenth century (Gotthard, Furka and Oberalp passes) and the railway tunnel opening in 1882, the Gotthard area became a highly strategic outpost. Fortifications in the region underscored this fact and were thus regularly adapted. Defence of these Alpine fortifications reached its apex during the Second World War as the backbone of the National Reduit strategy, with the Gotthard at the very core of the defensive measures implemented.

168 Dome turret for a cannon
October 2016
Gotthard Pass (Ticino)

174 Real emotions shape the future
June 2019
Sedrun (Grisons)
In the access gallery of the Gotthard Base Tunnel.

180 Tribute to the suffering of men
June 2018
Airolo (Ticino)
Displayed in Airolo train station, this artwork by Ticino sculptor Vincenzo Vela pays tribute to the many victims of the construction of the first Gotthard rail tunnel. Conceived at the sculptor's own initiative in 1882, it was unveiled much later, in 1932, for the fiftieth anniversary of the tunnel's opening.

PHOTOFOLIO II

6 Dawn at Furka Pass
September 2019
Furka Pass (Uri)
The blue hour at the Furka Pass, in a world of silence, with a sublime view of the Bernese Alps.

185 The Vanished Glacier
September 2018
Furka Road (Valais)
See p. 37 for the same view a hundred years earlier.

186 Gletsch and the Old Hotel Seiler
Glacier du Rhône
September 2019
Gletsch (Valais)
In Gletsch, located at what was the end of the valley at the time, the Seiler family built an inn which opened in 1862 and offered rest to travellers who wanted to admire the Rhône Glacier, as well as respite to the horses and coachmen who brought them there. The Furka Pass, which became practicable in 1867, and Grimsel Pass a few years later, ensured Gletsch years of glory. The later development and opening of the valley, greater mobility of motorists and the glacier's retreat resulted in the Seilers abandoning the inn in 1984.

187 Ospizio km 5
September 2018
Gotthard Pass (Ticino)

188 Customs and roadwork house
August 2019
Stelvio Pass (Italy)

189 First snowfall
September 2019
Oberalp Pass (Grisons)
A surprise first snowfall of the season can occur in the Alpine passes as early as September. Such is the case here at Oberalp Pass, 2046 m., in 2019.

190 Hotel
June 2021
Furka Pass (Valais)
From Realp in the canton of Uri, to Gletsch in the Valais, the road offers a truly breathtaking Alpine panorama. Approaching Gletsch, there used to be a spectacular view of the Rhône Glacier, within easy reach at the time.

With the development of tourism in the nineteenth century, the Hotel Seiler opened in Gletsch in the 1850s and the Hotel Belvédère was built in 1882 on the road to the Furka Pass (see p. 36). In 1964, the actor Sean Connery stayed here during the filming of the movie *Goldfinger*. Later, however, as the Rhône Glacier retreated over time, the legendary hotel lost its appeal and eventually closed its doors.

191 The Origen Theatre at Julier Pass
January 2021
Julier Pass (Grisons)
Origen means genesis, origin or creation in the Romansh language, Switzerland's fourth official language. Under the impetus of the Origen Cultural Foundation, a tower was constructed at the Julier Pass in 2017, which both separates and connects the country's major language regions. A four-year programme was unveiled honouring the year-round artistic expression of this trilingual region which thrives on cultural interaction. The ephemeral tower is slated to be dismantled in autumn 2023.

193 1914–1918 War Memorial
June 2019
Umbrail Pass (Grisons)
When Italy, an ally of Austria and Germany since 1882, suddenly realigned itself with the Allies and declared war on Austria during the First World War, a ruthless war of attrition was fought in the high Alps. The Swiss border at Umbrail Pass, protected by the army, was the scene of a fierce confrontation, with artillery positions at 3,850 m. above sea level on Ortler peak, opposite Stelvio Pass.
In memory of these tragic events, the Stelvio Umbrail Association erected a monument at the top of the Umbrail Pass. Present-day South Tyrol and Trentino devolved to Italy by the peace treaty of 1919.

194 Diavolezza Panorama
June 2021
Bernina Pass, Diavolezza (Grisons)
Arriving at the Diavolezza mountain hut by cable car, visitors spontaneously go outside, regardless of the weather, to admire the Alpine range stretching from Piz Palü to Piz Morteratsch and Piz Bernina, which on this particular day is hidden by clouds.

195 Descending
June 2019
Nufenen Pass (Ticino)
Although it is the day of the summer solstice, the snowy residue of winter at 2,000 m. makes for a setting that this cyclist will not soon forget.

196 The Totensee in fog
August 2020
Grimsel Pass (Valais)

198 Furka Pass and quote from a letter written by J.W. Goethe in Switzerland in 1779
August 2020
Furka Pass
"I observe that in my notes I make very little mention of human beings. Amid these grand objects of nature, they are but little worthy of notice, especially where they do but come and go." (translation A.J.W. Morrison).
The erstwhile Hotel Furka was built on this promontory (see p. 32). It was demolished in 1982.

199 Val Tremola
September 2020
Gotthard Pass (Ticino)
The Tremola is the name of the well-known sinuous road that leads through the valley of the same name from Airolo in Ticino up to the Gotthard Pass. The Tremola road has largely been preserved in the same state of reconstruction completed in 1951, and is supported by walls of up to eight metres high. It was originally built between 1827 and 1832, when the road was constructed as far as Göschenen to provide a link between Chiasso and Basel.

200 Santa Maria Dam
September 2018
Lukmanier Pass (Grisons)
Goats find cool and nourishing pasture at the foot of Santa Maria Dam, completed in 1968.

201 Monolith
September 2020
Grimsel Pass (Bern)
A magnificent monolith in the forest above Handegg.

202 Avalanche cone
June 2019
Umbrail Pass (Grisons)
Although it is already the month of June, the avalanche cones from the past winter are still visible. They are a reminder of the difficult climatic conditions at this elevation, where avalanches are the greatest risk. This is the main reason for the closing of the passes in winter. Very few of them remain open year-round.

203 Aare Gorge
September 2019
Innertkirchen (Bern)
The Aare Gorge lies at the bottom of the Grimsel and Susten Passes in the Hasli Valley in the Canton of Bern. The lower part of the valley is separated from the upper part by a natural hard limestone barrier called the "Kirchet", which resisted the crushing glaciers during the Ice Age. It was only when the glaciers receded that water was able to cut its way through the limestone, creating the Aare Gorge which, in certain places, is only about one to two metres wide.

204 Construction site of the new Spitallamm dam
September 2020
Grimsel Pass (Bern)
Construction of the Grimselsee Dams was completed in 1932. The larger Spitallamm wall needed restoration due to a crack that appeared in the 1960s. In the end it was decided to build a replacement dam with a double bend in front of the existing wall, which was to remain. Due to the short clement season at this altitude, work is already well underway before daybreak.

206 Morning light on the Finsteraarhorn
September 2020
Grimsel Pass (Bern)
A view above the Grimselsee on the Finsteraarhorn, 4,274 m., and the Agassizhorn, 3,953 m.

207 Seven days in Switzerland...
September 2019
Nufenen Pass (Valais)

215 Grimsel Pass (Bern)
August 2019
Richard de Tscharner at Grimsel Pass, photograph by Roger Oltramare.

258 Graffiti
June 2019
Umbrail Pass (Grisons)

HISTORICAL MAPS

MAP 1

MEDIEVAL TRADE ROUTES IN SWITZERLAND

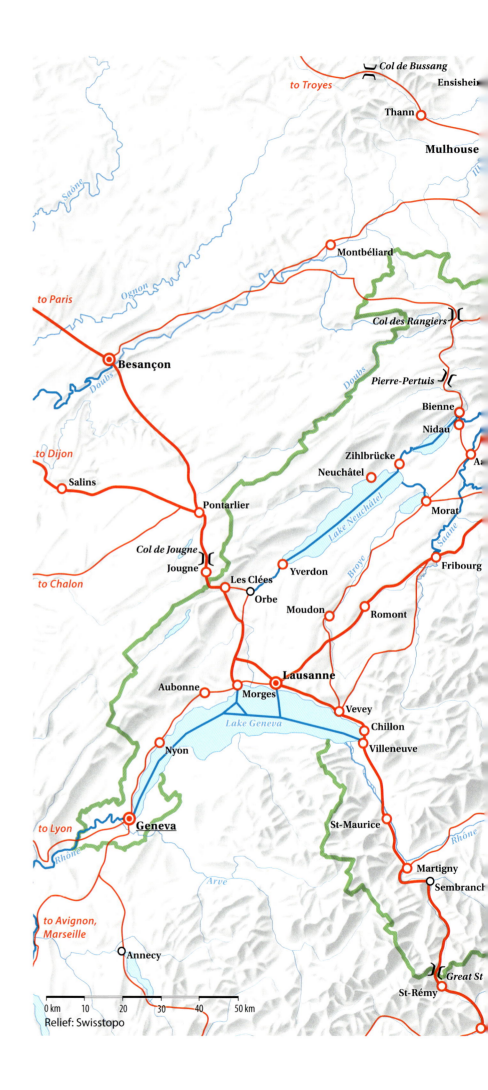

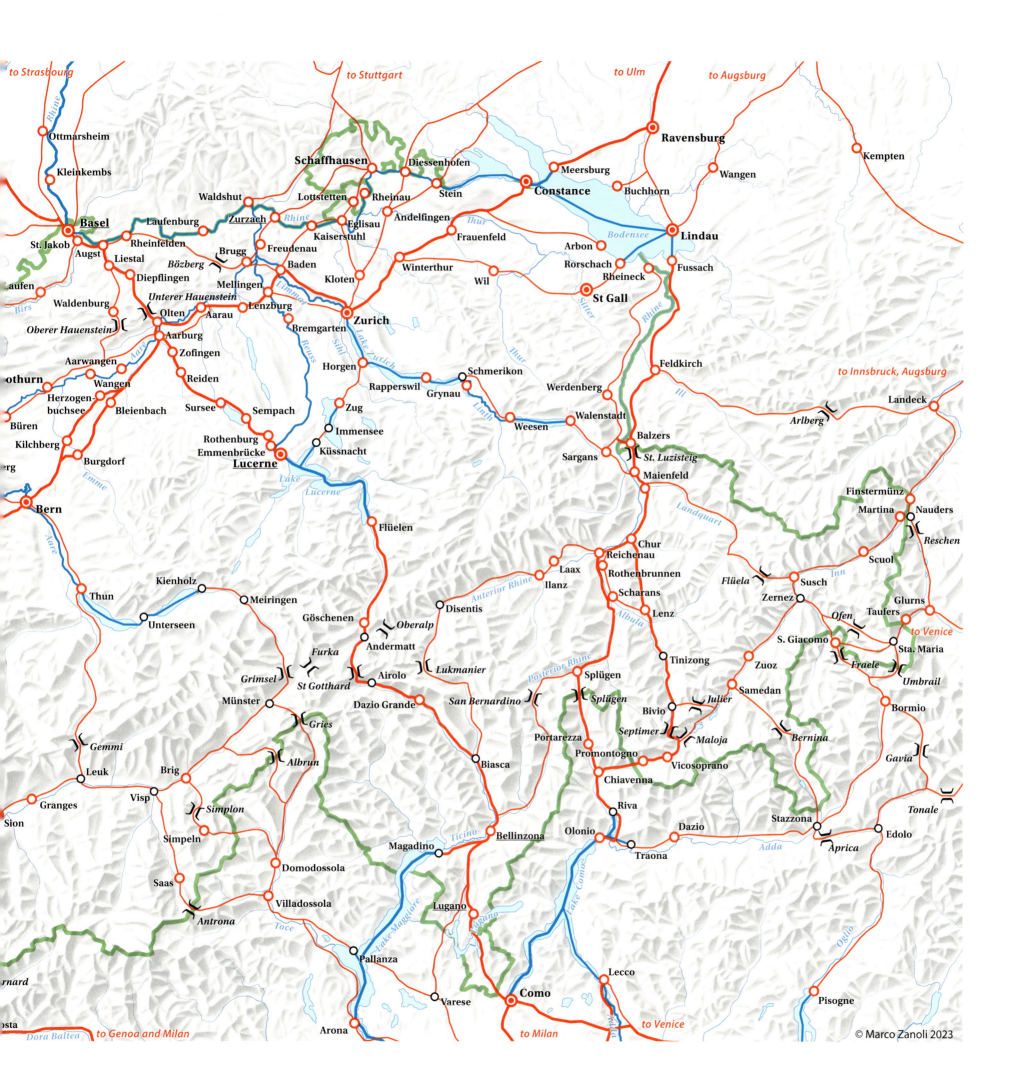

MAP 2

THE SWISS CONFEDERACY 1385

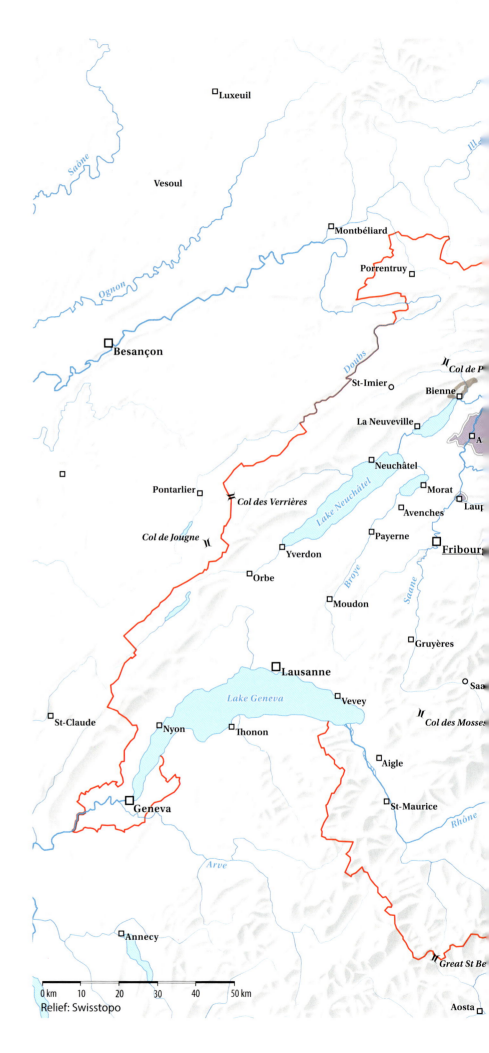

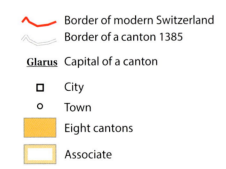
Border of modern Switzerland
Border of a canton 1385
Glarus Capital of a canton
□ City
○ Town
Eight cantons
Associate

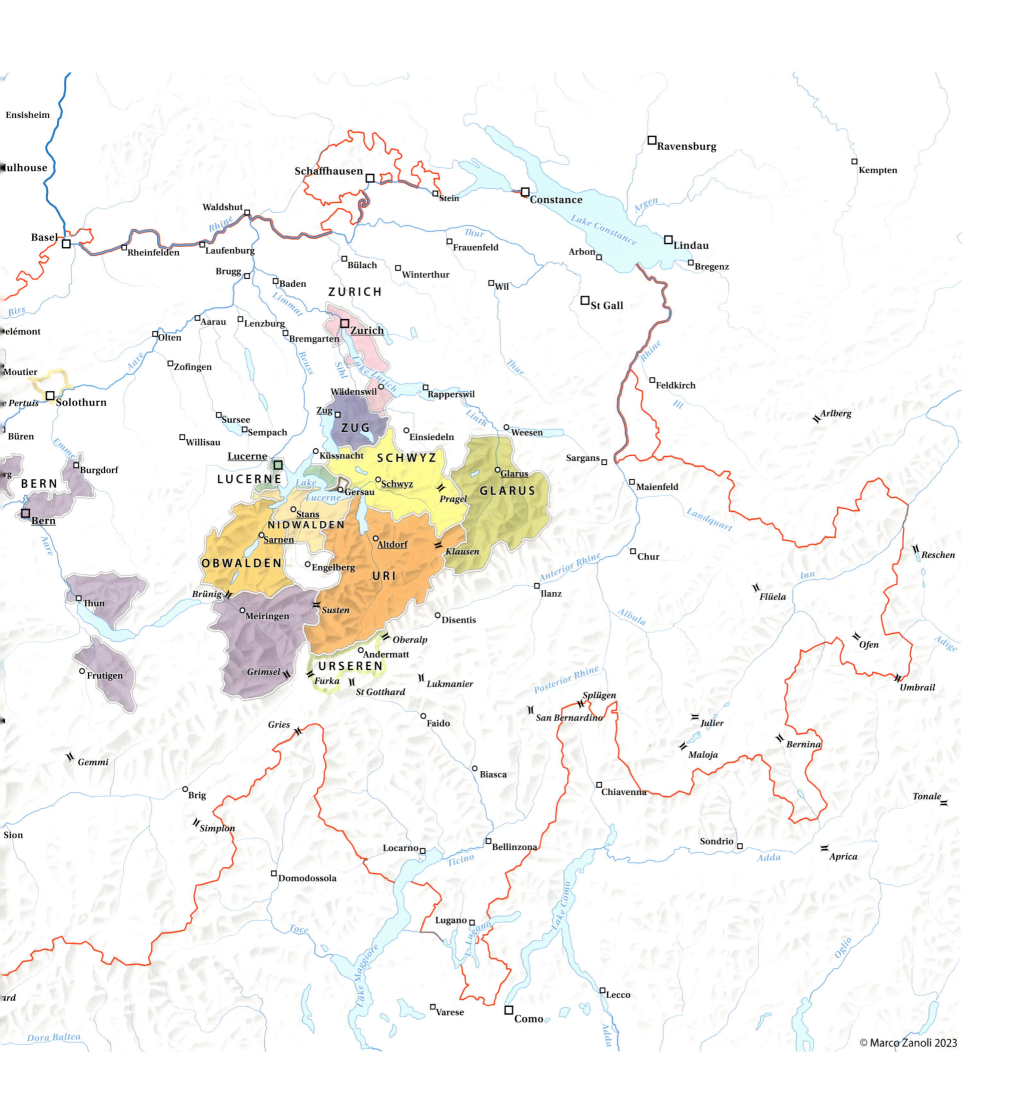

MAP 3

TRANSMONTANE BAILIWICKS

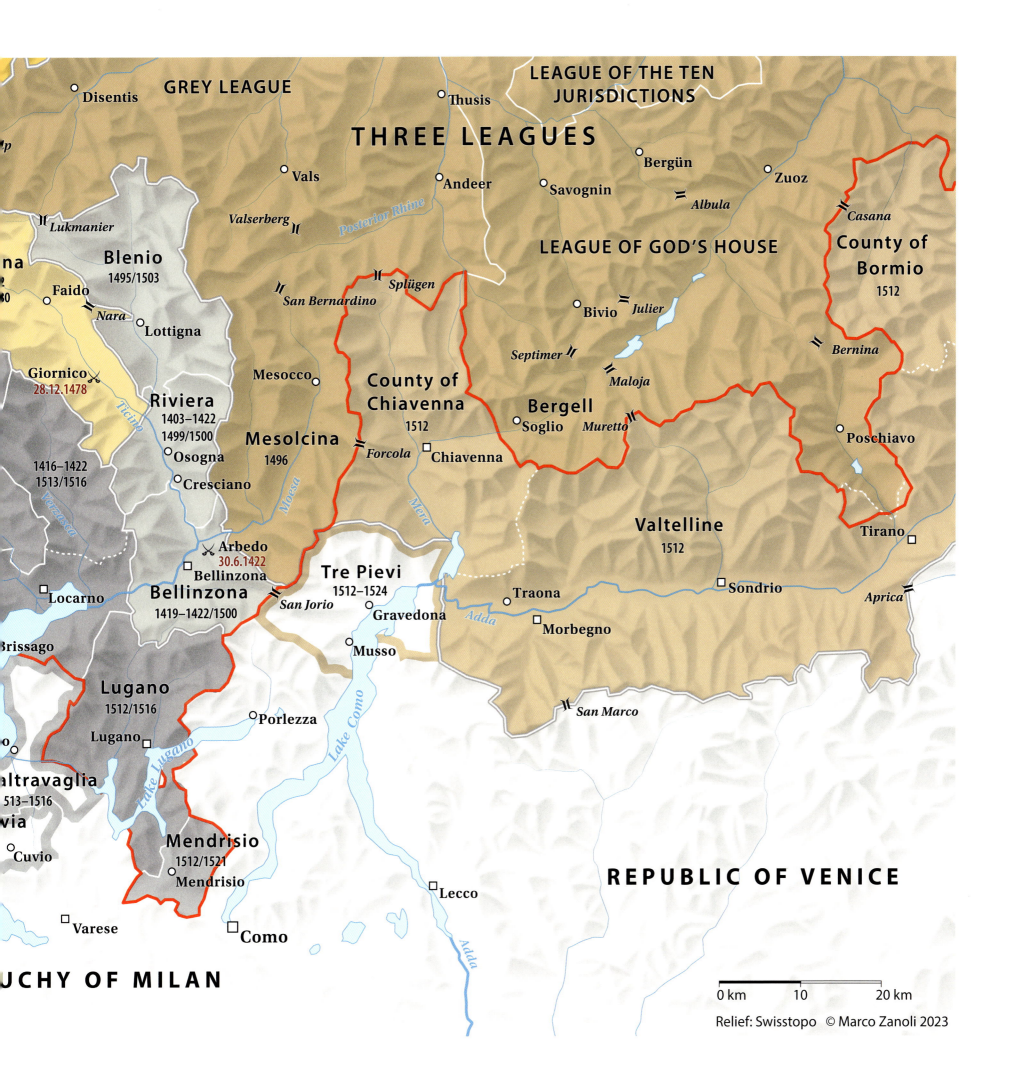

MAP 4

THE SWISS CONFEDERACY 1515

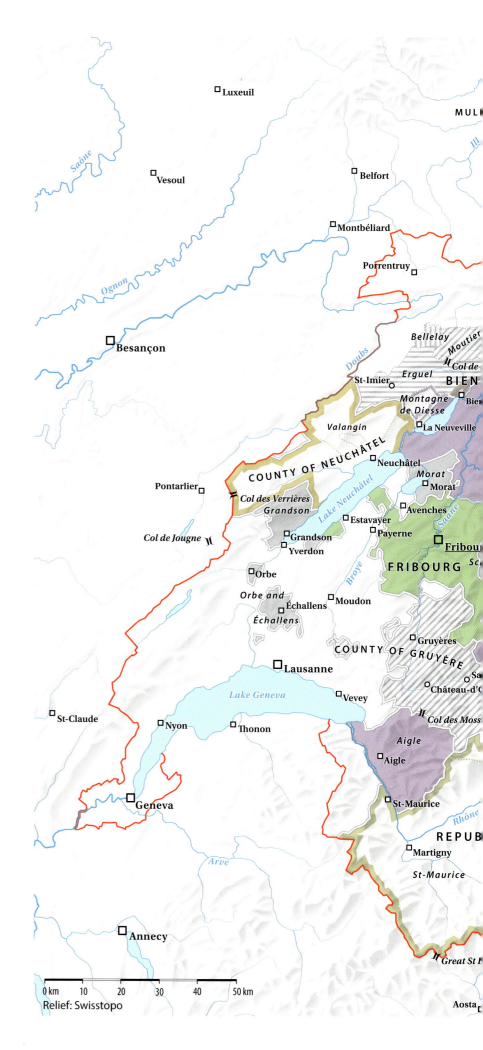

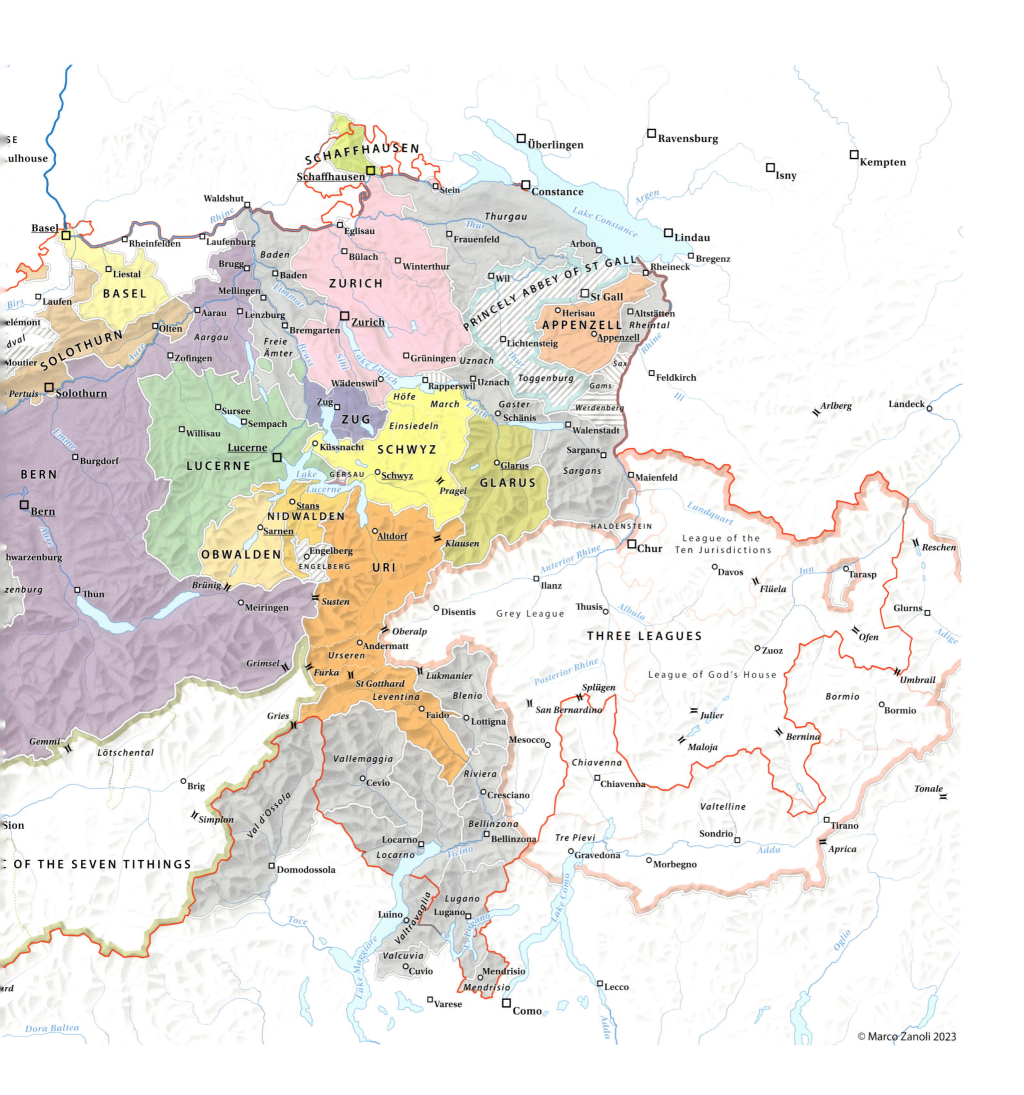

MAP 5

REVOLT OF THE LEAGUES: 1st PHASE 1620–1622

- Habsburg territory (Spain/Austria) 1620
- Territory of the Three Leagues 1620
- Ceded to Austria/Spain 1622 (Treaty of Milan)
- Spanish/Austrian campaign
- Campaign of the Three Leagues
- Campaign of Bern and Zurich
- Fortification
- Pass
- Battle

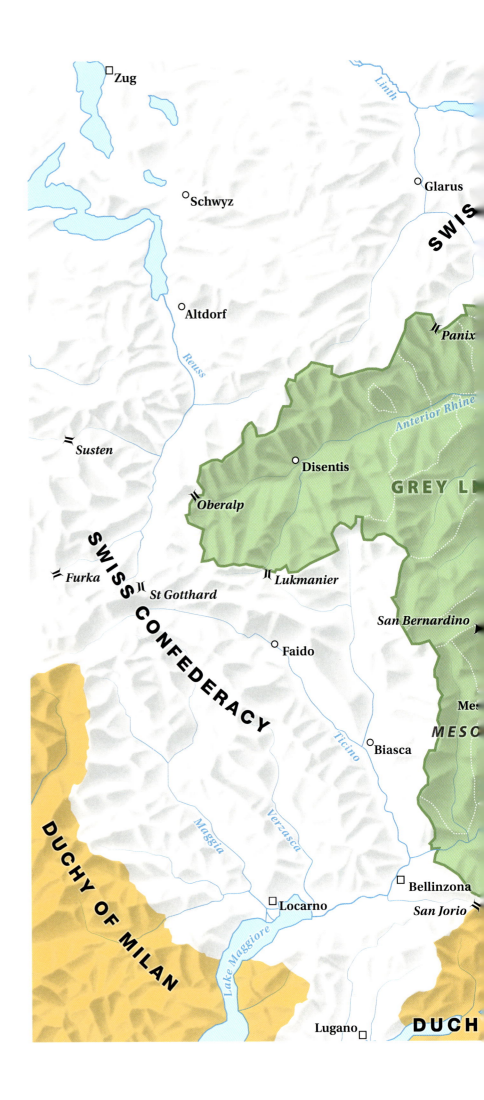

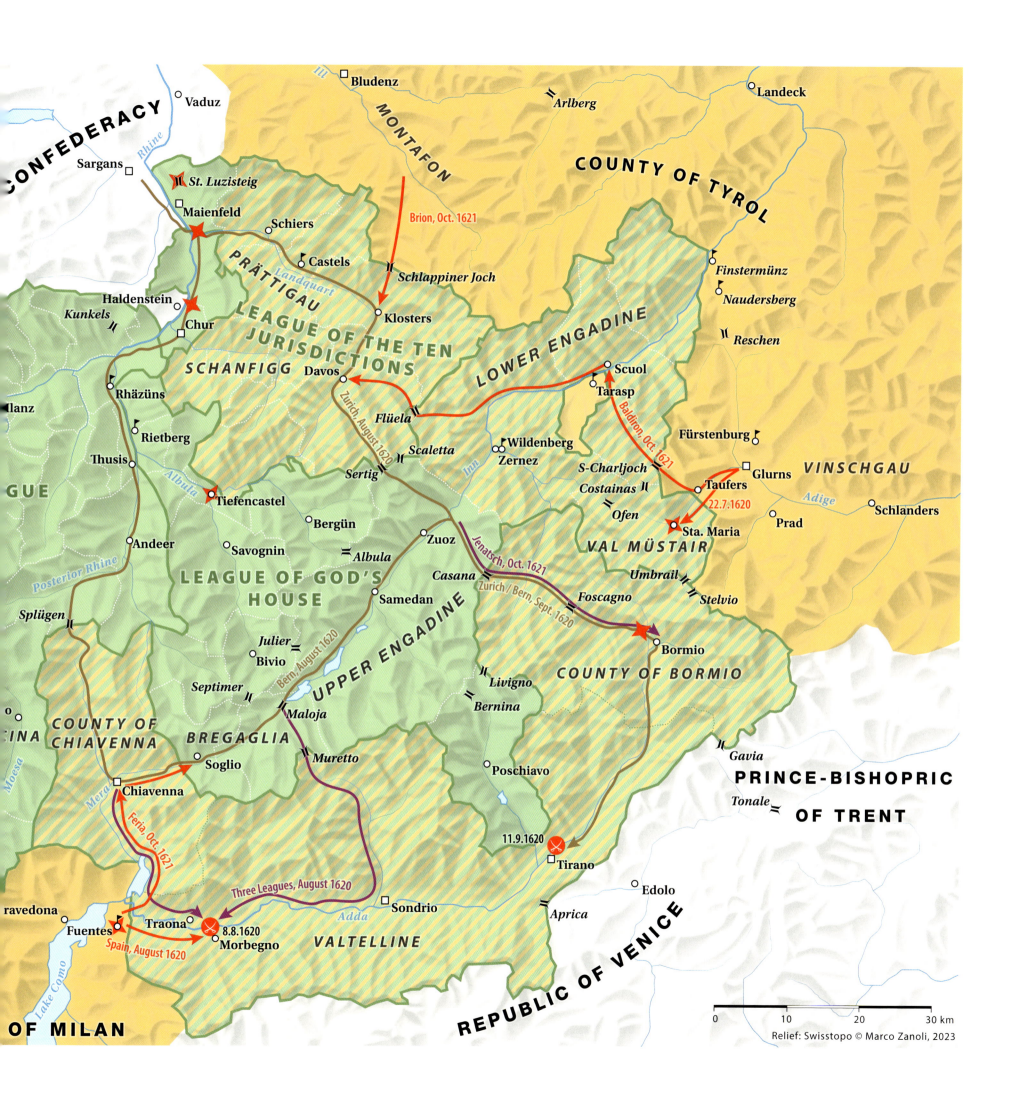

MAP 6

REVOLT OF THE LEAGUES: 2nd PHASE 1622–1626

- Habsburg territory (Spain/Austria) 1622
- Territory of the Three Leagues 1620
- Ceded to Austria/Spain 1622 (1626 returned to the Three Leagues)
- → Spanish/Austrian campaign
- → Campaign of the Three Leagues
- → Campaign of the Allies under French command
- ★ Fortification   Pass   Battle

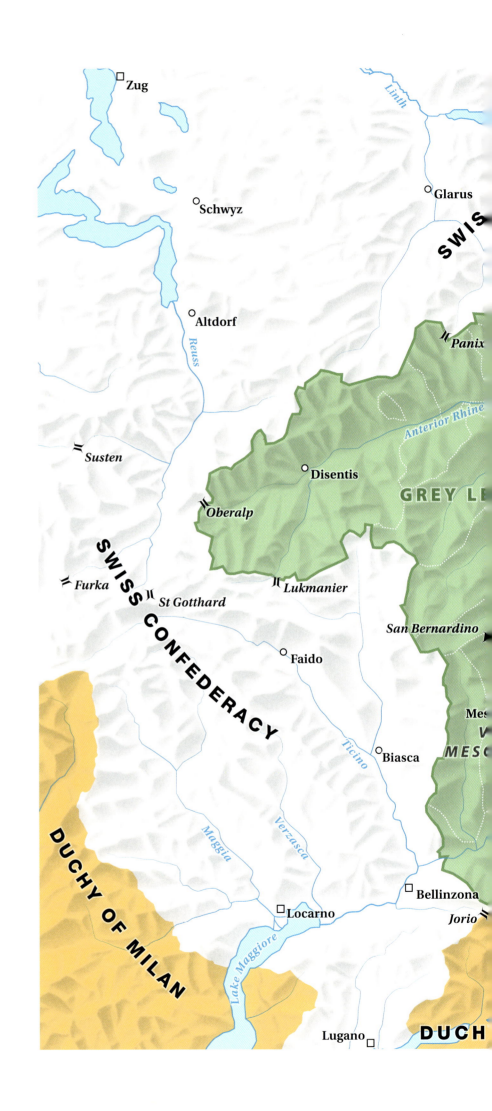

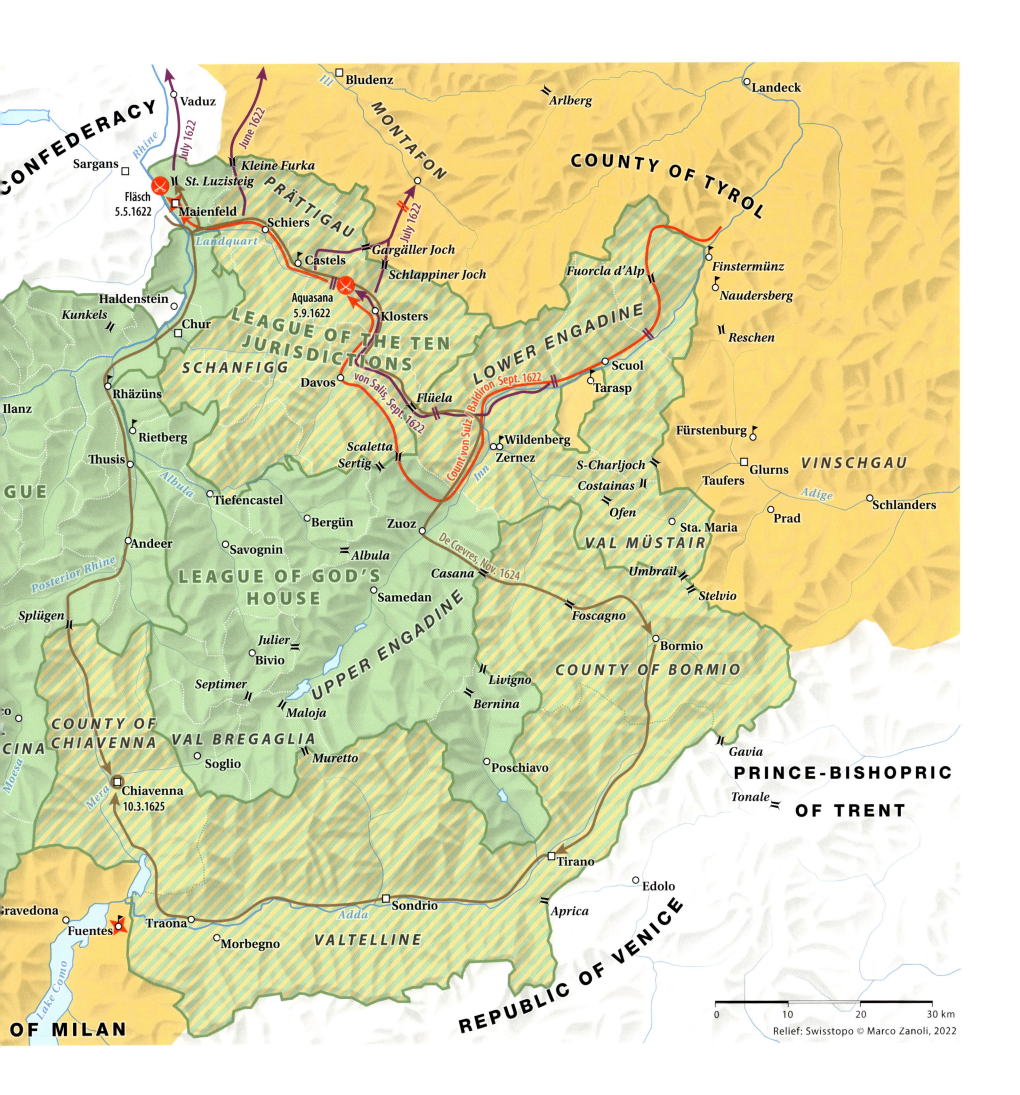

MAP 7

REVOLT OF THE LEAGUES: 3rd PHASE 1635

- Habsburg territory (Spain/Austria) 1635
- Territory of the Three Leagues 1635
- Territory subject to the Three Leagues
- Spanish/Austrian campaign
- Campaign of the Allies under French command
- Fortification
- Pass
- Battle

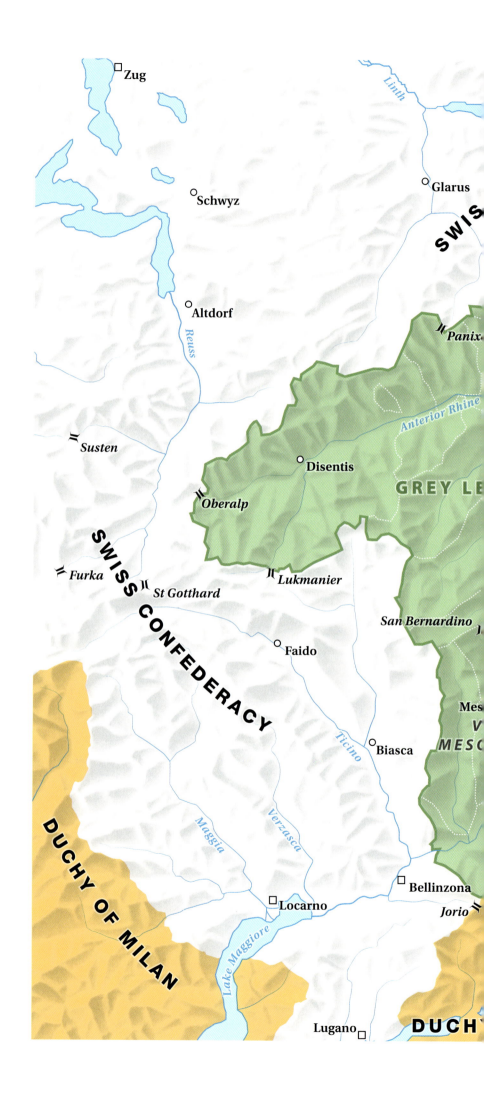

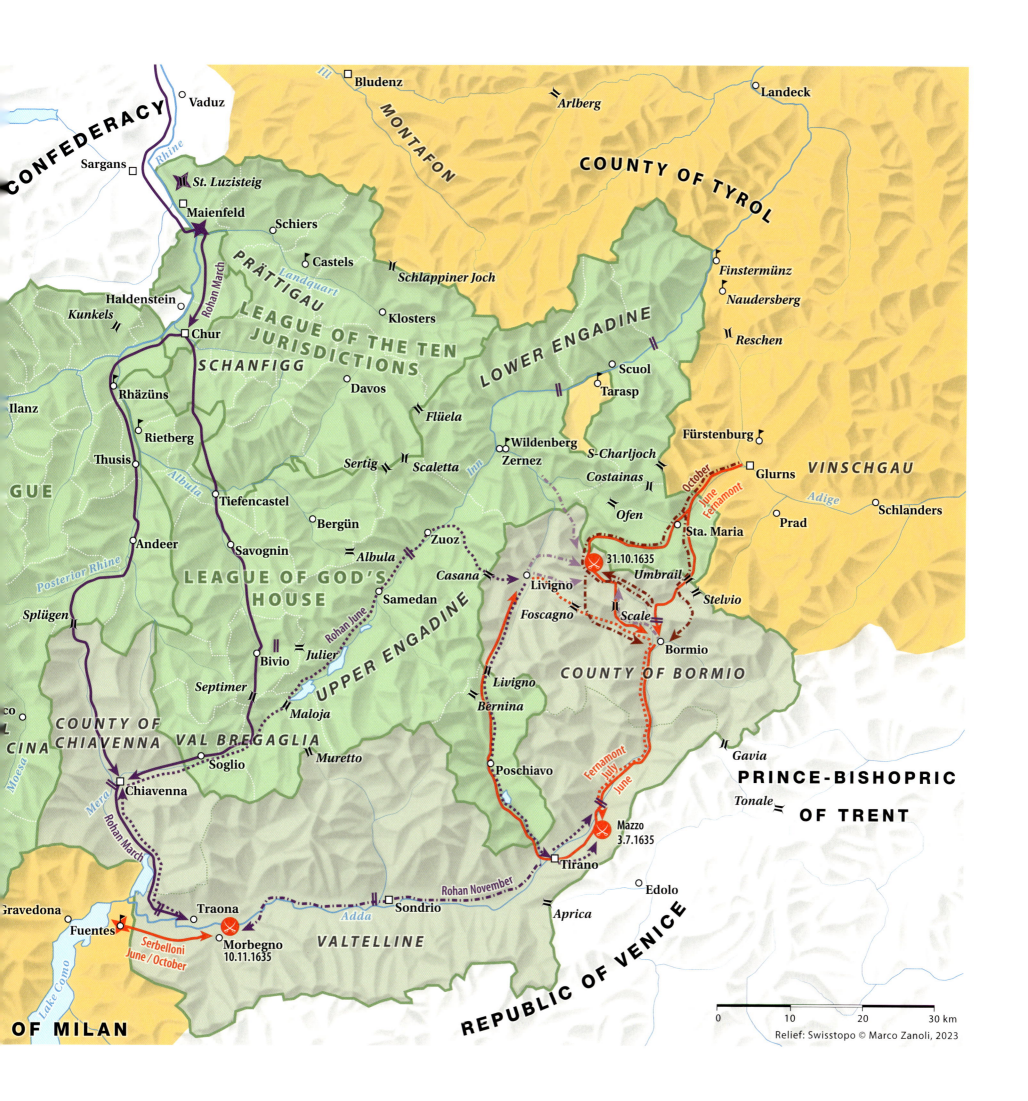

MAP 8

ALPINE REDUIT PLAN 1940

- International border 1939
- Border position
- Advanced position
- Central area
- Fortification
- Fortress
- General command headquarters
- Army corps command post 1939
- Army corps command post 1941

MAP 9

SWITZERLAND 2022

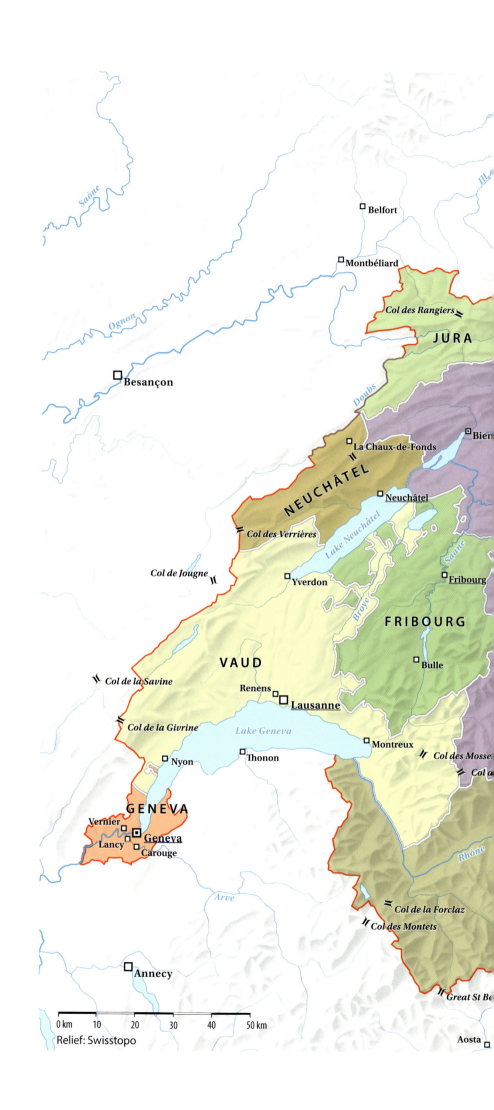

—	Border of modern Switzerland
—	Border of a canton 2022
<u>Sion</u>	Capital of a canton

City (population 2020)
- ▣ over 200 000
- ☐ over 100 000
- ⊡ over 50 000
- ▫ over 20 000 (selection)
- ○ Town (selection)

Abbreviations
- AI Appenzell Inner Rhoden
- AR Appenzell Outer Rhoden
- BS Basel City
- BL Basel Country
- LI Liechtenstein

246

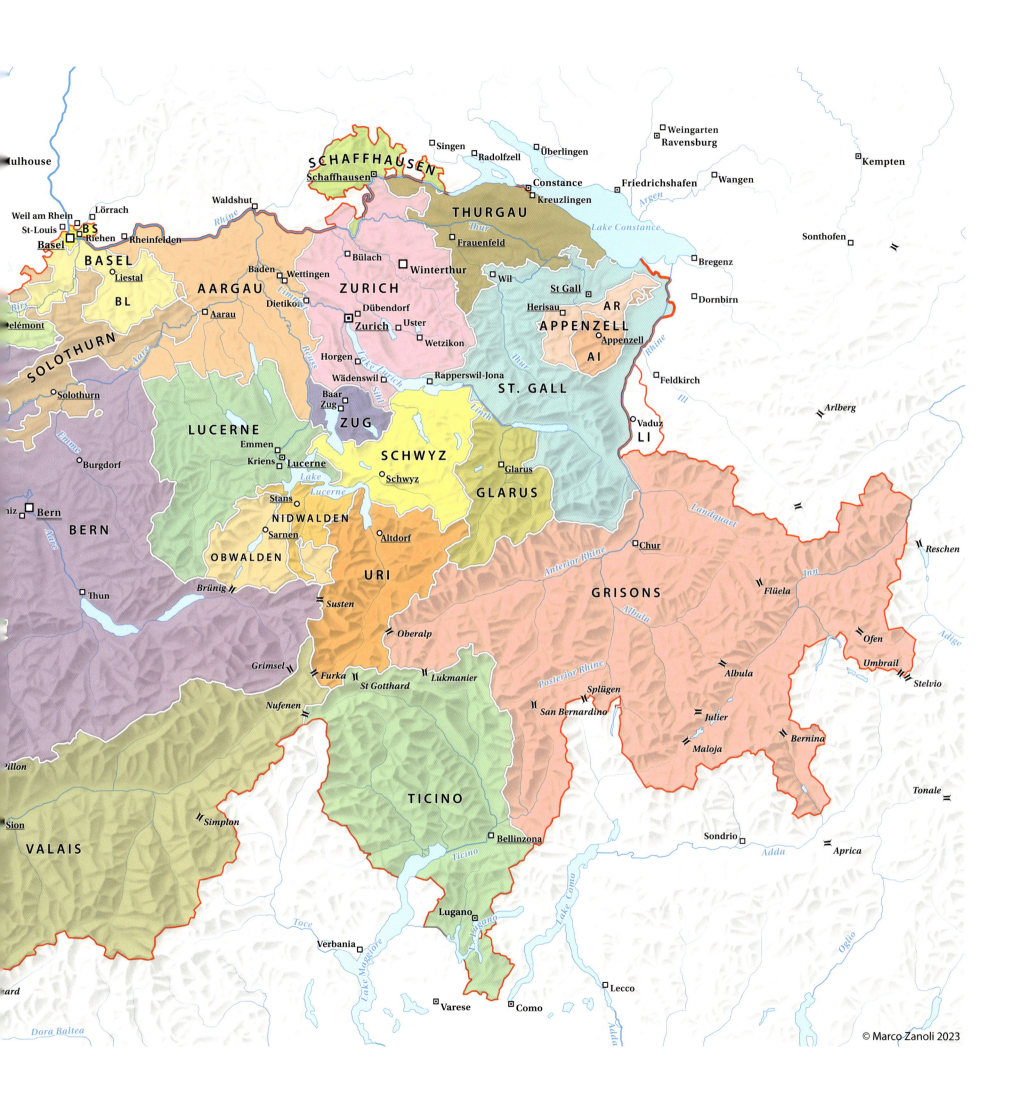

CONTRIBUTORS

Frédéric Möri

Frédéric Möri was born in Paris in 1971. He earned a PhD in ancient philosophy before devoting his life to teaching, photography and writing. Humanism and its essence are his core interests. Focusing on the knowledge that human beings have acquired and passed on, he seeks to convey the essential importance of human dignity across centuries and cultures.

His first major work was *Le chant intérieur* (2002), for which he undertook a several months-long photographic immersion study of contemplative monks, designed to approach as closely as possible the "reality" he had studied for his dissertation on Neoplatonic and early Christian ontology.

He subsequently conceived, realized, illustrated and produced two exhibitions and two publications for the Martin Bodmer Foundation in Geneva: *Orient-Occident* (2009) and *Alexandrie la Divine* (2015). On these occasions, he designed and chaired two international academic seminars on the transmission of knowledge in Greco-Roman, Jewish, Christian and Muslim cultural spaces, from Antiquity to the Renaissance. In relation to these endeavours, he worked in coordination with numerous well-known scholars and in partnership with renowned cultural and scientific institutions.

In constant quest for meaning, Frédéric Möri is currently engaged in a photographic portrayal of nurses and palliative care workers in various hospitals in French-speaking Switzerland. Based on first-hand testimonies and personal encounters, this delicate mission seeks to convey the utmost significance of human dignity.

Daniel Lätsch

Brigadier (Ret'd) Daniel Lätsch was born in 1957 and grew up in Rüti, in the canton of Zurich. He completed a commercial apprenticeship in the textile machinery industry before studying general history, military history and English literature at the University of Zurich (1982–1988). In 1994, he obtained a PhD in military history.

In 1989, he joined the Professional Officers Corps and was initially posted to the Infantry School at St Gallen. In 1996, he graduated from the British Army Staff College in Camberley. After assignments as a tactical instructor at the Infantry Officers School in Zurich, commander of basic studies at the Military Academy at the Swiss Federal Institute of Technology (ETH) and course manager for the Army XXI project team, he took over leadership of the Infantry Officers School in Zurich. Promoted to Brigadier in 2004, he was appointed Commander of Infantry Brigade 7. From 2006 to 2011 he led the Military Academy at ETH Zurich, and from 2012 to 2017 the General Staff School.

As a militia officer, Daniel Lätsch was assigned to the Zurich Mountain Forces, commanding Regiment 37. As a general staff officer, he served on the staff of Fest Br. 13 and Geb Div. 12.

The author of numerous articles and book contributions on security policy and military issues, Daniel Lätsch also leads military history study tours.

He is married, has a daughter and a son, and lives in Jona.

Anton Affentranger

Anton Affentranger was born in Argentina in 1956, of Spanish and Swiss descent. He grew up in Peru, Chile and Switzerland, and holds a degree in economics from the University of Geneva.

For the first twenty years of his professional career, he was an investment, corporate and private banker in New York, Hong Kong, Geneva and Zurich. Switching to the other side of the negotiating table, he became an entrepreneur and built an investment platform and several technology start-ups and businesses. He is one of the founders of Implenia, Switzerland's leading construction and real estate firm, where he served as chairman and CEO for over a decade.

In recent years, the consequences of climate change have become Anton's primary concern. His entrepreneurial activities and actions today focus on making a positive impact on the health of our planet.

Anton Affentranger has been an enthusiastic marathon runner for years. This discipline and what it takes to run a marathon typify qualities he values.

In 2018/19, he travelled around South America for six months. This journey took him from the glaciers of the Antarctic to the high plains of the Argentine, Bolivian and Peruvian Puna, and then to the Amazon Forest. Its beauty and the progressive deforestation observed, together with the distances and lasting impressions of this entire expedition, inspired deep reflection on life's fundamental questions about "being" or "not being". During this journey, he wrote his book *Baustellen* (Construction Sites).

Anton Affentranger is married to Melinda. They have two adult sons and live in Zurich.

Richard de Tscharner

Richard de Tscharner was born in 1947 in Bern, Switzerland, where he spent his youth. He then moved to Geneva where he obtained a university degree in economics and the social sciences. In 1972, he joined the Geneva-based private bank Lombard Odier & Cie, where he worked for thirty-four years and was appointed managing partner in 1989.

Richard de Tscharner retired from the financial world – and business travel – in 2006. A nature lover, he took to travelling with his photographic equipment. In 2008, he embarked on a 108-day journey around the world, staying mainly off the beaten track. This experience changed his worldview and was the inspiration for his first photography book, *Our World*, published in 2009. An exhibition in Geneva followed the year after.

Other expeditions followed, often to places far removed from civilization, where man can encounter himself, but also venture in search of the traces of time and the paths of our planet's journey through time. Richard de Tscharner seeks out those landscapes still untouched by mankind, whose sole purpose is to express the beauty of the world, the Deep Time of our planet, as opposed to the Short Time of human existence. This approach led to exhibitions near Geneva in 2015, at Sotheby's in Geneva in 2017, in Italy in 2021 and Zurich in 2022.

Since 2017, Richard de Tscharner, his wife and their two daughters have lived in Dubai.

CARÈNE FOUNDATION

CARÈNE FOUNDATION

Guy Vermeil, Member of the Board

Promoting Education, Preserving Tradition

Today's knowledge has been transmitted to us by the scientists, artists and builders who came before us. The inestimable legacy we have inherited and of which we are the depositaries must be preserved and transmitted in turn to future generations. The commitment to educational values has inspired Richard de Tscharner to work towards promoting the transmission of knowledge and cultural values in the interest of their preservation and nourishing cultural dialogue.

To this end, he created the Carène Foundation in 2008. Based in Switzerland, the Carène Foundation is governed by Swiss law. It is recognized as a non-profit organization serving the public good by the Federal Authority for Monitoring Foundations of the Swiss Confederation and donations by benefactors residing in Switzerland are tax-exempt. As custodian of the photographic archives of its founder, the Carène Foundation is the sole beneficiary of his photographic work.

Foundation Board members share a passion for culture, art and photography, thereby enabling the Foundation's support for the following:

- conservation of the manuscripts in the library of St Catherine's Orthodox monastery in the Sinai, to preserve the valuable cultural roots of humanity

- the Order of Malta, represented in Cambodia by the CIOMAL Foundation (Order of Malta International Campaign Against Leprosy), in its advocacy and early detection against leprosy campaigns

- the Cape Haitien Historical and Heritage Preservation Society, for the preservation of the historical archives of the Court of First Instance in Cap Haitien, endangered by the 2010 earthquake

- the Martin Bodmer Foundation in Cologny, near Geneva, funding all expenses linked to the photographic content of the *Alexandrie la Divine* exhibition and two-volume book

- the Factum Foundation for Digital Technology in Preservation and its study of the cultural importance and challenges to preserving the Bakor monoliths in Cross River State, Nigeria

- the Bourbaki Panorama Association in Lucerne, in safeguarding a monumental circular painting depicting the French army crossing the border led by General Bourbaki on 1 February 1871 at Verrières. More than 87,000 soldiers were disarmed, given asylum, fed and otherwise taken care of in Switzerland, in an immense expression of humanitarian solidarity that was in essence the first mission of assistance provided by the then recently founded Red Cross.

The Carène Foundation's commitment to educational values led to its support of the Karuna-Shechen Association in Tibet and the Krousar Thmey Association in Cambodia. In Nepal, responding to the desolation caused by the 2015 earthquake, the Carène Foundation and the Ustinov Foundation, together approved the construction of the private Him Shikhar Carène Ustinov School, honouring the efforts of two devoted Swiss benefactors thanks to whom the village of Nele, situated in a remote valley in Solukhumbu district, was fully reconstructed.

In 2023, it is thus an honour for our Foundation to publish this book on Alpine passes in Switzerland, places of both separation and convergence, and of passage, forever bearing witness to the evolution of our country's history. These passes are inextricably linked to the genesis and evolution of the Helvetic Confederation and today's Switzerland, its borders and ultimate configuration. We are proud to preserve and transmit the cultural heritage of our Alpine passes.

ACKNOWLEDGEMENTS

ACKNOWLEDGEMENTS
Richard de Tscharner

What began as a photographic expedition over time developed into a work on Swiss Alpine passes and their role through the ages in shaping the country that is Switzerland today. I am grateful to all the contributors and proud of the excellent team with which it has been my privilege to collaborate. Each contribution, from the authors and translators, revisors, copyeditors, technicians and advisors, not all of whom could be named here, has been significant in its own right to this collective endeavour.

I would like especially to acknowledge:

Doris Leuthard, Swiss Federal Councillor (2006–2018), for her enthusiasm, spontaneity and commitment to this project in such a personable and warm manner

Frédéric Möri, whose insight, vast culture, knowledge and inimitable writing style offer a most valuable foundational account of the historical and philosophical significance of the passes

Daniel Lätsch, Brigadier (Ret'd), historian and military expert, for his remarkably focused and comprehensive editorial on the strategic role of the Alpine passes

Anton Affentranger, for having accepted, as former chairman of Implenia, to recount the genesis and construction of the Gotthard Base Tunnel.

I also wish to thank:

William A. Ewing, member of the board, Carène Foundation, and curator of the Foundation's photography collection, historian and internationally acclaimed photography expert, with whom it is always a pleasure to embark on a new photographic adventure

Douglas Parsons, my faithful collaborator for nearly twenty years, for the perfection of his prints

the institutions that have graciously opened their archives and provided the historical photographs in this book: Nicolas Crispini Collection, Geneva; ETH-Library, Zurich, Image Archive; Keystone-SDA, Bern/Photopress Archive/Jules Decrauzat; Swiss Alpine Museum, Bern; Sammlung Fotostiftung Schweiz, Winterthur; Bruno Bischofberger Gallery, Meilen; Swiss National Library, Bern, Federal Archives of Historic Monuments, Photoglob-Wehrli Archives; Swiss National Museum, Zurich

Bernard Stackelberg, "my" graphic designer ; translators, revisors and copyeditors Nina Vugman, René Haenig and Laetitia Guggi; and my advisor Chantal Oltramare, for their enthusiasm and highly qualified professional engagement,

my beloved wife Laetitia and our daughters Lily and Luna, with all my heart, for their love, understanding and infinite patience during the many hours I spent away and behind my desk.

Graffiti – Umbrail Pass (Grisons)

IMPRINT

EDITOR: Carène Foundation / Richard de Tscharner

CONCEPT: William Ewing, Frédéric Möri, Richard de Tscharner

TEXTS: Anton Affentranger, Daniel Lätsch, Doris Leuthard, Frédéric Möri, Richard de Tscharner

TRANSLATION GERMAN – ENGLISH: Susan Jacquet, FRENCH – ENGLISH: Nina Vugman

COPYEDITING: Douglas Parsons

PROOFREADING: Sarah Quigley

PHOTO EDITING AND PRINTING: Douglas Parsons, PhotoRotation SA / Olivier Oberson

MAPS: Marco Zanoli

COORDINATION: Nadine Olonetzky

DESIGN: Sixty-six Communication Design / Bernard Stackelberg

PRINTING: Genoud Arts graphiques, Le Mont-sur-Lausanne

BINDING: Schumacher AG

© 2023 Verlag Scheidegger & Spiess AG, Zürich
© for the texts: the authors
© for the images: Richard de Tscharner
Other photographic credits: Nicolas Crispini Collection, Geneva: pp. 16, 75 — ETH-Library Zurich, Image Archive: pp. 24, 25, 28 Edit. Schroeder & Cie, p. 31 Edit. Photoglob, pp. 65, 80 — © Keystone-SDA/Photopress Archive/Jules Decrauzat: p. 36 — © Roger Oltramare: p. 215 — © Swiss Alpine Museum: pp. 61, 62, 68, 79 — Sammlung Fotostiftung Schweiz : p. 41 © 2022 Bruno Bischofberger, Meilen, pp. 52, 76 — Swiss National Library, Federal Archives of Historic Monuments, Archives Photoglob-Wehrli: pp. 21, 22 — Swiss National Museum: p. 15 (LM-805336/GBE-39182), p. 27 (LM-100169.26/GBE-13710), p. 32 (LM-101478.35/DIG-14154), p. 33 (LM-101401.78/DIG-7986), p. 37 (LM-91058.1/GBE-133895), p. 55 (LM-116483.4/ROH-2289) Studio PDL-Fotoagentur Presse Diffusion Lausanne, p. 56 (LM-79763.75/GBE-125330), p. 72 (LM-146474.7/GBE-45631), p. 73 (LM-170958.19/DIG-48419)

Verlag Scheidegger & Spiess AG
Niederdorfstrasse 54
8001 Zurich
Switzerland
www.scheidegger-spiess.ch

ISBN 978-3-03942-162-6

All rights reserved; no part of this publication may be reproduced, stored in a retrieval system or transmitted in any form or by any means, electronic, mechanical, photocopying, recording or otherwise, without the publisher's prior written consent.

Scheidegger & Spiess AG is being supported by the Swiss Federal Office of Culture with a general subsidy for 2021–2024.